To my beautiful Brazilian wife, Rita Pierotti-Madden, who generously pours love into my life, sprinkles it with cinnamon, and keeps me organized—which is not easy.

To my daughter Adrienne, who keeps asking me to polish the news releases our interns write.

To my daughters Angela and Robin, who are always lifting my spirits; and to my son, Andrew, whose resilient, lofty spirits seldom need a lift.

WORDSHINE MAN

Tips for Polishing Words UNTIL THEY SPARKLE

TOM MADDEN

Once shoes, now words need polish,
hence the Wordshine Man cometh.

You want words to tell her you love her?
But not so many that'll smother?
Here's what I advise you, brother:
go see the Wordshine Man.

Once scuffed, dirty shoes needed polish.
Nowadays it's words won't shine.
So I tell you, bro, consult a word pro.
Go see the Wordshine Man.

A magician with words is he.
Reels 'em out with glee, not free.
You slap some grease in his hand,
and he's yours, the Wordshine Man.

Prose he comes up with will scintillate.
She'll know you're her number-one fan.
Never too late for love to percolate.
Go see the Wordshine Man.

He prefers present tense, puts wordy behind a fence.
Keeps it nice and tight, tells verbose: "Take a hike!"
Nothing too flowery, not on his salary.
Got a message to deliver? He'll rev his motorbike.

He's the Wordshine Man!

INTRODUCTION

In earlier days, it was just our scuffed, dirty shoes that needed polishing, so we went to a shoeshiner. They were often called shoeshine boys because the job was traditionally done by a male child.

Nowadays it's our words, sentences, and paragraphs in those news releases, articles, media pitches, letters, proposals, and blogs we struggle to write that need polishing—that need the Wordshine Man to come do his thing.

After decades of performing public relations feats; winning awards and accolades; founding one of the nation's top PR firms, TransMedia Group, whose past and current clients over the last forty years comprise a who's who of America's greatest, most successful companies and organizations, from AT&T to the City of New York; who has launched a slew of start-up businesses, making their owners rich and famous, in some cases billionaires, through blitz after blitz of meteoric publicity; who has won countless recognitions and top awards, including the Bronze Anvil from the Public Relations Society of America; Tom Madden, this entrepreneur and old tiger CEO, has graduated to a new sacrosanct position at his award-winning PR firm. He's become TransMedia Group's Wordshine Man!

Every day at TransMedia Group's world headquarters in Boca Raton, Florida, you'll see Madden showing an army of college interns and young recruits how to write hard-hitting, attention-getting news releases, media pitches, letters, and other forms of PR content.

Sure, today's young college graduates might be bright, bursting with ideas, digitally inclined, ambidextrous, and speedy as they peck away at their smartphones and laptops, but putting words together in a logical, attractive way that clearly and emphatically makes a news release cry out for attention, and writing it with purpose and effect always seems to need polishing—Maddenesque polishing.

No, you can't write with just your thumbs going a mile a minute as you do on your iPhone or Android. You need to put your mind, body, and spirit into the process—into that erstwhile art called writing.

So in writing this book, *Wordshine Man*, you're seeing what has become of the illustrious founder of the PR firm TransMedia Group. He's now a shiner of words, sentences, headlines, and verbally—the kitchen sink.

Yes, Mr. Madden graduated from CEO to Wordshine Man. This is what he's asked to do more and more these days—polish, polish, polish—as we have a herd of fresh interns and raw recruits "helping" us, who often need emergency help themselves.

"Dad, can you polish this release one of our interns wrote?" texts Adrienne, my industrious daughter who is president of our firm, where ofttimes I'm now not just CEO but the all-hours writing coach and word polisher in chief.

In this book are a series of real before and after examples of how to make writing more engaging. By simply adding, deleting, or rearranging a few words, a writer or editor can make even dingy, lackluster prose shine and inspire action. Isn't that what most commercial writing is supposed to do?

That's what Madden does as the Wordshine Man when he's not blogging (www.MaddenMischief.com), appearing on television and podcasts, or pitching media himself. He polishes. And he polishes. And he polishes. And there are never any tips!

Yes, this time around it's not polishing shoes, but words.

FROM HERE COMETH MY LOVE FOR WORDS

I fell in love with words while confined to a hospital bed for eight eternally long weeks after I foolishly broke my neck one summer day lifeguarding in Atlantic City, NJ—everyone but myself!

It was a silly, almost slapstick diving accident while I was a young lifeguard at the popular Traymore Hotel where my dad played the violin and my mom ran our talent business, the Convention Entertainment Bureau, which booked musicians and acts for parties and events.

That fateful day after work, I took my lifeboat out into the surf for a muscle-building row. To cool off afterward, I dove into the ocean onto what, unbeknownst to me, was a sneaky sandbar that had been hiding ominously below, lying in wait—for my neck!

Wonderful! I broke and dislocated my fifth and sixth cervical vertebra. Goodbye, that summer!

I spent it suspended by hooks in my skull, lying flat on my back in the hospital in a striker-frame bed, whereupon I took up reading the complete works of witty Irish playwright, George Bernard Shaw: *Pygmalion, Major Barbara, Saint Joan, The Devil's Disciple*, et cetera.

Ironically, I had cut high school one year, thumbed a ride down to Miami, and got a small part playing a very young General Burgoyne in *The Devil's Disciple* at the Coconut Grove Playhouse. The director told me as an actor I had a great sense of timing, but I guess it wasn't working that day when I dove into the ocean. Lying there in the hospital, I read all of Shaw's books cover-to-cover upside down through prism glasses. The glasses enabled me to read his books while resting them on my chest, as I could only look straight up at the ceiling. In the aftermath of that death-defying dive has come a torrent of words shooting out of me in five books, a slew of speeches, and so many news releases, published articles and blogs, I can't even count.

I told this neck-breaking story the other day to the actor Andres Perez-Molina, known for *Last Call at Murray's* (2016) and *No Ordinary Family* (2010). During his illustrious Hollywood career, Molina has played supporting roles in such major motion pictures as *The Dark Night Rises, La La Land*, and the 2009 *Star Trek*, as well as recurring roles in such television shows as Netflix's *Disjointed* and CBS's *Code Black* and *The Mentalist.* He has also co-starred in the Amazon Prime series *The Marvelous Mrs. Maisel* and *Goliath.*

He was enthralled with my cervical story, as not too long ago he injured his C2 in a fall, and like me was nearly paralyzed from the neck down, spending weeks in a wheelchair. Thankfully, like me, he, too, fully recovered.

My daughter Adrienne and I invited him to join our talent agency, Madden Talent, and do some PR for him while he's taking care of his mother in nearby Parkland. When selling our PR services, I always try to find something in common with the person whom I'm pitching.

So Andres and I had what you might call a spinal connection.

In *Wordshine Man: The Spin Man*, the title of one of my previous books, I demonstrate how to give your writing a spit shine that will make it stand out and generate news or whatever you're seeking to accomplish. So watch the Wordshine Man in action and see how you can almost instantly turn dull, placid prose into sparkling, engrossing writing!

I'm talking to some colleges and universities—including my alma mater, the Annenberg School of Communications at the University of Pennsylvania—about supplying to graduate students this badly needed writing handbook on how to wordshine.

Start making your words not just readable but prolific, powerful, and incendiary. Become a self-polisher, a verbal catalyst, a luminary, an inspirer, and even an agitator, if necessary. So, just like the Wordshine Man, be your own wordsmith!

CHAPTER 1

A DAY IN THE LIFE OF THE WORDSHINE MAN

Here is a snapshot of a day in the life of the Wordshine Man and what he goes through at all hours—day after day, night after night—wordsmithing for his capricious clients, changing their words, adding hyphens, rephrasing their sentences, and correcting news releases ad nauseam. If you want to be a prose polisher, you'd better get your act together. Get used to wordshining until the cows come home, which is a trite expression you should avoid like the plague—another tired expression that's "old hat."

The phone rings.

It's a call from Greg close to midnight. He says to put the release on the newswire at 11:00 a.m. It's the same release already rewritten four times! So early the next morning, he receives an email: "Greg, just so I wasn't dreaming when I got that late-night call from you last night, this is to confirm that you want the attached to go out on the newswire at 11:00 a.m. today and not before the market opens, as Jack wants?"

Before getting back to sleep to finish polishing that dream I was having before Greg called, there's an urgent email from Susan telling me that her partner, Syd, doesn't like the word "loft." She meant "lofty" in front of "principles," so could I please change it. Quickly message her back: "Okay, Susan, in lieu of 'lofty,' how about simply 'highest' or 'topmost?' Sydney built a world class ARM organization, inserting the highest principles into process and performance. 'My dedication was always to the people I hired,' he said."

Yikes! "World class" isn't hyphenated, so the sleepless, now bleary-eyed wordsmith tells Susan he just noticed "world class" needs to be hyphenated as "world-class." Good night!

And on and on it goes, ad infinitum, as the clichés keep flying higher and higher.

In the interest of full disclosure, you must know Madden is a mad blogger. He calls his blog *MaddenMischief.* Why? Because he's pretty mad these days. And he doesn't mind doing a little mischief on people's minds if it will wake them up and shake them into thinking differently about themselves and about events happening in our culture. If he can get them to snap out of their traditional ways of pigeonholing minorities, Republicans, or liberals and open them to new thoughts, feelings, and perspectives on liberty and that oddity called democracy, he'll sleep better.

If he's not chortling over the absurdity of current events, poking fun and satirizing them, he's plain pissed about the dumb dissention that keeps dividing America. Some call him the modern Howard Beale, the fictional character from the film *Network* (1976), who billed himself as the Mad Prophet of the Airwaves.

Beale exhorted his TV network viewers to stick their heads out of their windows and yell at top of their lungs one of the most iconic lines in film history: "I'm as mad as hell, and I'm not going to take this anymore!"

After feeling irritated and sick to my stomach over the presidential election slugfest, I'm fuming over the postelection's paralyzing politics and a new brand I call "pillow politics." Here cometh the Mad Prophet of the Blogwaves.

Dare read what I yell at the top of my lungs out of my internet window about these unrelentingly senseless and raucous political seasons, how we incite and condone riots, and hold impeachment after impeachment.

Here are some recent samples from *MaddenMischief*:

"AS IF THERE'S NOT ENOUGH POLITICS, HERE'S ONE YOU CAN TAKE TO BED, BUT DON'T EXPECT TO SLEEP: PILLOW POLITICS."

Unhappy with the MyPillow guy, Mike Lindell, supporting former president Trump, and David Hogg are ready to start a pillow fight in the first round of pillow politics.

And with Tuesday comes the ultimate pillow fight: an attempt by pillow-armed Democrats to smother any chance for Trump to ever become president again. They'll be betting on another impeachment long shot.

Democrats are going to have to prove that expressing free speech near a mob that makes them angry is the same as shouting, "Fire!" in a crowded theater.

Trump's fiery words were these: "If you don't fight like hell, you're not going to have a country anymore."

March For Our Lives cofounder David Hogg tweeted he and software developer William LeGate are launching a competitor to MyPillow.

MyPillow CEO Lindell is one of former president Trump's most ardent defenders, who has repeatedly shared unsubstantiated conspiracy theories about the presidential election.

Lindell had a tumultuous interview with Newsmax recently, during which anchors tried to block the CEO from reiterating conspiracies about the 2020 election, but he refused to lie down and kept swinging his pillow at them. Dominion Voting Systems also sent a cease and desist letter to Lindell last month, ordering him to preserve all documents related to the company.

Lindell told news media he wants Dominion to "put up or shut up" their lawsuit because he claims there's "100 percent evidence that China and other countries used their machines to steal the election," even though the US Department of Justice has found no evidence to support Lindell's claims about Dominion Voting Systems or any widespread voter fraud.

Hogg said he and LeGate hope to "sell $1 million of pillows within the first year," and they expect to enter the pillow ring in about six months.

Lindell's response? "Good for them . . . nothing wrong with competition that does not infringe on someone's patent."

Now that's no feather talk from the unruffled MyPillow CEO.

BRADY POWER

I rooted for Tom Brady last night, but he didn't seem to need too much encouragement to win his seventh Super Bowl. It was a piece of cake.

Back in 2017, I wrote a book about the 2016 presidential election and how President Trump was then putting his White House in order so he could carry out his promise to "make America great again."

That was not a piece of cake.

That book, which is still circulating today and is available on Amazon, is titled *Is There Enough Brady in Trump to Win the inSUPERable Bowl?*

Why Brady?

Back then, Trump was down in the points, behind in the polls, and I was asking rhetorically whether our forty-fifth president could pull off a *huuuuuuge* win to fulfill his promise—his well-promoted promise.

I thought of how amazing and dramatic Brady was at coming from behind and pulling out those Super Bowl wins.

The book was a compilation of my *MaddenMischief* blogs during and right after the 2016 election—some of them intending to warn Trump that maybe he should tweet less, govern more, and apply some Brady power.

CHAPTER 2

HOW TO WRITE A PRESS RELEASE THAT WON'T DIE ON THE VINE ONLINE

To get right down to the nitty-gritty, what follows are a series of actual "before-and-after" examples of news releases and other forms of writing that will demonstrate how changing a few words can give a news release greater influence, make it more readable, and garner an editor's interest in running the story.

What follows are not complete releases, only the most important parts: the headline and the first few paragraphs. If they don't catch the attention of an editor, reporter, or TV news director or producer right off the bat, you're sunk.

In this first "Before" are the makings of a headline grabber, but it's weak and needs a transfusion in the form of a biblical saying, as you'll see in the "After." Check it out.

BEFORE

"UVC-650" PleXus Device Effectively Sanitizes Mosaic Church of COVID-19

In lieu of the pandemic, PleXus UVC-650 is ending the year 2020 keeping patrons of Mosaic Church in Winter Garden, Florida safe. PleXus is extremely effective in sanitizing large spaces where COVID-19 and other viruses, germs and infections lurk.

So many in various genres of community gatherings have suffered greatly during the "stay in place" orders that a machine such as PleXusUV that kills 99.98% of the virus is helping the social distance gatherings such as Church re open.

"We have many good deeds that need to get done and with PleXus, we were able to continue on with our mission," said Isaac Rodrigues, Director of Facilities, Mosaic Church. "I like that it's easy to maneuver and quick as theirs more time used in helping others," added Rodrigues.

AFTER

Believing Virus Cleanliness Is Next to Godliness, PleXus's 'UVC-650' Sanitizes Mosaic Church of Satanic COVID-19

PleXus UVC-650 is ending the year 2020 keeping patrons of Mosaic Church in Winter Garden, Florida, religiously safe. PleXus is the light that's extremely effective in sanitizing large spaces where COVID-19 and other viruses, germs, and sinful infections lurk.

So many in various genres of community gatherings have suffered greatly during the stay-in-place orders that warrant a machine such as PleXusUV, that kills 99.98 percent of the virus, helping social distance gatherings such as a church reopening.

"We have many good deeds that need to get done, and with PleXus, we were able to continue on with our mission," said Isaac Rodrigues, director of facilities, Mosaic Church.

"I like that it's easy to maneuver and quick to allow more time to help others at this grave time," added Rodrigues.

BEFORE

Mirai Clinical Launching Fabric Spray Like Never Before

Mirai Clinical (https://miraiclinical.com) presents the Deodorizing Fabric spray, a unique product made with Japanese Persimmon. Senior care facilities and gyms can benefit from our odor remover spray as it works well in removing the distinct smell that comes with age as higher oxidation rate of lipids is observed among older people and people with higher testosterone levels.

AFTER

Mirai Clinical Launches Odor Remover Fabric Spray That Makes Elderly at Senior Care Facilities Smell Like They're Young Again

Mirai Clinical (miraiclinical.com) presents the Deodorizing Fabric spray, a unique product made with Japanese persimmon that can peal the years away. Senior care facilities and gyms can benefit from our odor remover spray as it works well in removing the distinct smell that comes with age as higher oxidation rate of lipids is observed among older people and people with higher testosterone levels.

BEFORE

NB Natural Encourages You to Switch to Natural Skin Care on National Science Day

NB Natural is celebrating this National Science Day by encouraging everyone all around the country to go through their skin care products. NB Natural is a bioscience skin care brand that uses Nobel Prize-winning technology to help actively repair your skin.

AFTER

In Honor of National Science Day, NB Natural Encourages You to See If Your Skin Care Products Are Science-Backed and Natural

NB Natural is celebrating this National Science Day by encouraging everyone to go through their skin care products to see if they're backed by science. NB Natural is a bioscience skin care brand that uses Nobel Prize-winning technology to help actively repair your skin.

BEFORE

Rise and Shine. It's Hunting Time! Today's Restaurant News Will Be Sponsoring The SkyClip Scavenger Hunt

Now let's do that over, keeping in mind this time that The Sky-Clip is a device that holds your cellphone and papers security clipped to your tray table when you fly.

AFTER

Time to Find What's Missing When You Travel. Join the SkyClip Scavenger Hunt Sponsored by Today's Restaurant News

Next we have what are called agency rosters, which are releases in which a public relations firm can announce a new client on the newswire, but done in a way that will get attention and attract media interest. At least, that's the objective.

BEFORE

> **NB Natural Looks Back On Stellar 2020 with New Products, New Events and New Series**
>
> Despite COVID-19 affecting many small businesses across the U.S., NB Natural Powered by Nourishing Biologicals (nbnatural.com) created new skincare products, launched new projects, and even gave back to their Saint Augustine community throughout 2020.

Okay, now let's see if we can't polish this a bit, starting with a crisper headline. The goal is to tighten the prose, which means saying as much in fewer words. Why would you start out by saying something we already know—that the virus has affected many small businesses? Let's skip the bun and start with the meat!

AFTER

> **What a Stellar 2020 for NB Natural, Encompassing New Products, Unique Events, and a TV Series to Boot**
>
> COVID-19 didn't stop NB Natural, powered by Nourishing Biologicals (nbnatural.com), from creating fine skin care products, launching new projects, and giving gave back to their Saint Augustine community throughout 2020.

Do you see how we can make news more attractive by just adding an element or two like saying a fabric spray doesn't just smell nice but makes seniors feel young again.

Next, we're going to place words on a stretcher and carry them into the word emergency room for the wordshine doctor to examine the most vital part of any news release—the beginning, or what's known as the headline.

BEFORE

BOCA RATON, FL—All are welcome to join in a discussion with abortion rights attorney, Rabbi-rouser, and former legislator Rabbi Barry Silver tonight (Friday, September 3rd) at 8:00 PM EST at his weekly Zoom and Schmooze event.

AFTER

BOCA RATON, FL—While Texas legislature firing squad takes aim at women's rights, all are welcome to join in a discussion with abortion rights attorney, Rabbi-rouser, and former legislator Rabbi Barry Silver tonight (Friday, September 3rd) at 8:00 PM EST at his weekly Zoom and Schmooze event.

BFORE

Science-Fiction Author Edgar Scott's *'418: I Am A Teapot'* Now In Store at Boca Raton Barnes and Noble, Limited Signed Copies Available

AFTER

Science-Fiction Author Edgar Scott's *418: I Am a Teapot* Has Landed From Outer Space In Store at Boca Raton Barnes and Noble Where Signed Copies Loom

CHAPTER 3

HEADLINE GRABBERS

Now let's look at the all-important headline—the grabber. If your headline doesn't grab readers' attention, you're cooked. We've all heard that first impressions are important. Well, that's what the right headline does for your message.

Headlines are hand extenders, as if they're extending a welcoming hand to the reader to come aboard and read your work. It's like you're offering to shake hands with someone whom you've just met or to whom you're being introduced.

Here's a headline about a public company announcing financial results, but it's missing two words that will make it go from flaccid and anemic to hitting the first-impression jackpot. The key words "Outpacing 2019" belong in the headline.

BEFORE

OriginClear Maintains Its Momentum in Third Quarter

OriginClear Inc. (OTCQB: OCLN), The Water Company for the New Economy™, announces that revenues and gross profits for the first nine months of 2020 continued to outpace the same period in 2019.

AFTER

OriginClear Maintains Momentum in Third Quarter, Outpacing 2019

OriginClear Inc. (OTCQB: OCLN), the Water Company for the New Economy™, announces that revenues and gross profits for the first nine months of 2020 continued to outpace the same period in 2019.

BEFORE

Greg Breunich Named CEO of Altitude International Holdings

Altitude International Holdings, Inc. (OTCQB: "ALTD") announced that Greg Breunich has become its new Chairman, CEO and CFO. ALTD's prior Chairman, CEO and CFO, Bob Kanuth, will continue to be an integral part of ALTD's executive management team and will continue serving as a member of its Board of Directors.

Greg Breunich is an innovator at the highest levels of athletic performance and training. He began his career in 1978 working with Hall of Fame tennis legend Nick Bollettieri, who trained developed and coached superstar tennis champions.

Now look what happens when you add a catchy description of the company in the headline and a quote in the now livelier body of the release.

AFTER

Greg Breunich Named CEO of Altitude International Holdings, a Leader in Training Athletes in Simulated High Altitudes

Altitude International Holdings, Inc. (OTCQB: "ALTD") announced Greg Breunich will be the new chairman, CEO, and CFO of the leading supplier of custom-built simulated altitude chambers, enabling athletes to achieve the highest levels of performance in training.

"I greatly appreciate the opportunity and responsibility that Bob and the ALTD board of sports luminaries are entrusting me with," said Breunich, an innovator at the highest levels of athletic performance and training.

Breunich began his career in 1978, working with hall of fame tennis legend Nick Bollettieri, who trained, developed, and coached superstar tennis champions.

It always invigorates writing when there's a news angle prominently displayed. Here's a new product announcement that concentrates on online jewelry stores.

What it misses is the news angle. Because it's in twenty-four-karat pure gold, unlike most jewelry, it not only glitters but appreciates in value!

That salient information is missing from the headline in the before version. The fact that it appreciates in value isn't mentioned until the end of the second paragraph. It's downright dull.

BEFORE

Maison Laurea Introduces 24K Gold Honeycomb Cufflinks

Artistry, passion and value are the leading components that reflect everything the name stands for.

The beginning of one's jewelry journey begins at www.maisonlaurea.com, where discriminating clients can build an exclusive jewelry portfolio with handcrafted 24K gold pieces, ranging from filigree cuffs, classic pendants, structural cufflinks and more that will not just impress, but appreciate.

AFTER

Maison Laurea Introduces Honeycomb Cuff Links You Can Wear Not Only to Impress But to Invest Since They're Solid Twenty-Four-Karat Gold!

Laurea introduces the honeycomb cuff link in twenty-four-karat gold that not only makes a glittering fashion statement but appreciates in value, as do other twenty-four-karat pieces by Laurea.

Honeycomb cuff links have polished edges and a raw center to showcase the pureness of the precious metal and traditional artisan craftsmanship for which Laurea is known. Laurea's jewelry is uniquely designed all in solid twenty-four-karat pure gold.

For the same online jewelry store, here are one-two polish punches: *one* stands for before, and *two* represents after, or pre- and post-headlines showing ways to make the products shine:

1. Maison Laurea Adds Twenty-Four-Karat Pure Gold "Bar" Necklace to Investment Jewelry Line
2. Step Up to Maison Laurea's Twenty-Four-Karat Pure Gold Bar Necklace, A Stunning New Part of Its Investment Jewelry Line

1. Maison Laurea's Debuts Investment Jewelry Line with Elegant 24L Pure Gold Diamond Lariat Necklace
2. You'll Rope Eyes in with Maison Laurea's Elegant Twenty-Four-Karat Pure Gold Diamond Lariat Necklace That Will Delight While Gaining in Value

1. Maison Laurea's Investment Jewelry Line Includes Twenty-Four-Karat Pure Gold Drop Necklace
2. Looking for that Drop Dead Look? Maison Laurea's Investment Jewelry Line Features New Twenty-Four-Karat Pure Gold Drop Necklace

1. Maison Laurea's Creates a Unique Investment Jewelry Line with Dog Tag Necklace
2. Maison Laurea Expands Unique Twenty-Four-Karat Gold Investment Jewelry Line With Desirable Dog Tag Necklace

1. Maison Laurea's Debuts Introduces a Pure Twenty-Four-Karat Pure Gold Sun Pendant Necklace as Part of Their Investment Jewelry Line
2. Maison Laurea's Debuts Pure Twenty-Four-Karat Pure Gold Sun Pendant Necklace As Part of Its Investment Jewelry Line to Impress While It Appreciates

Here are more before and after examples that show how adding or subtracting a few words can make a big difference in your writing.

BEFORE

TransMedia Group Announces Public Relations Efforts for Investigative journalist, Filmmaker and Medicine Consultant Maryam Henein

TransMedia Group (www.TransMediaGroup.com) has announced today that it has been named the public relations agency of record by Maryam Henein (www.maryamhenein.com), an investigative journalist, documentary filmmaker and functional medicine consultant.

AFTER

TransMedia Group to Produce and Prescribe PR for Maryam Henein, an Investigative Journalist, Filmmaker, and Medicine Consultant on Coronavirus

TransMedia Group to provide a triple-play PR program for Maryam Henein, whose eclectic career covers investigative journalism, documentary filmmaking, and functional medicine consulting, including on the topic of coronavirus.

NOW LOOK AT HOW A SOUPED-UP HEADLINE SHARPENS THIS STORY

BEFORE

Common myths and misconceptions of HRT (Hormone replacement therapy)

For men, there's a myth that testosterone replacement causes *prostate cancer*. What we know now is that although testosterone supplementation may contribute to the growth of an already established prostate cancer, there are no compelling studies that show that testosterone actually causes it. In fact, what we see is that when we increase levels of testosterone to normal levels using *bioidentical testosterone*, as opposed to synthetic forms, there seems to be a reduced risk for developing this cancer if it is not already established.

Another myth is that in men, testosterone therapy causes or worsens cardiovascular disease (Heart attack/Stroke). What we actually see is that *bioidentical testosterone* therapy actually reduces the risk of cardiovascular disease in men, including heart attack and stroke. Synthetic forms of testosterone replacement therapy are potent contributors to inflammation in the body and this form of testosterone is the form that contributes to the increased risk. Bioidentical forms, on the other hand, are more anti-inflammatory and typically lower these risks.

In women, there is a myth that hormone replacement contributes to breast cancer and heart disease. This was based on studies using synthetic versions of estrogen and progesterone. What we know now is that when we use bioidentical hormone therapy (BHRT), as opposed to synthetic hormones, these risks are reduced with concomitant improvements in bone density, energy levels, libido, anxiety, mental clarity, and urogenital atrophy associated with the natural decline in hormone levels.

The key point is that there is a significant difference in how our bodies process bioidentical hormones compared to synthetic hormones. Synthetic hormones are more likely to aggravate chronic disease states and increase systemic inflammation while bioidentical hormones tend to reduce this in our bodies. And since inflammation is a key driver of all forms of acquired disease, our goal is to help reduce inflammation in the body as much as we can. BHRT is an important tool we often recommend in our mission to improve healthspan and increase lifespan.

Timothy Hoffmeister DO

AFTER

Contrary to common myths and misconceptions, HRT (hormone replacement therapy) actually improves our health, not worsens it!

MYTH #1: Testosterone replacement causes *prostate cancer* in men.

FACT: What we know now is that although testosterone supplementation may contribute to the growth of an already established prostate cancer, there are no compelling studies that show that testosterone actually causes it. In fact, what we see is that when we increase levels of testosterone to normal levels using *bioidentical testosterone*, as opposed to synthetic forms, there seems to be a reduced risk for developing this cancer if it is not already established.

MYTH #2: Testosterone therapy causes or worsens cardiovascular disease (heart attack/stroke) in men.

FACT: What we actually see is that *bioidentical testosterone* therapy actually reduces the risk of cardiovascular disease in men, including heart attack and stroke.

Synthetic forms of testosterone replacement therapy are potent contributors to inflammation in the body and this form of testosterone is the form that contributes to the increased risk. Bioidentical forms, on the other hand, are more anti-inflammatory and typically lower these risks.

MYTH #3: In women, hormone replacement contributes to breast cancer and heart disease.

FACT: This was based on studies using synthetic versions of estrogen and progesterone. What we know now is that when we use bioidentical hormone therapy (BHRT), as opposed to synthetic hormones, these risks are reduced with concomitant improvements in bone density, energy levels, libido, anxiety, mental clarity, and urogenital atrophy associated with the natural decline in hormone levels.

KEY POINT: There is a significant difference in how our bodies process bioidentical hormones compared to synthetic hormones. Synthetic hormones are more likely to aggravate chronic disease states and increase systemic inflammation while bioidentical hormones tend to reduce this in our bodies.

Since inflammation is a key driver of all forms of acquired disease, our goal is to help reduce inflammation in the body as much as we can. BHRT is an important tool we often recommend in our mission to improve healthspan and increase lifespan.

Factually yours,
Timothy Hoffmeister, DO

So you can see that by energizing verbs and having them highlight the most important or most colorful points you can get a better grip on readers' interest and yank them into consuming the story. Remember: the more compelling the headline, the more successful the outcome!

CHAPTER 4

EMAIL SUBJECT LINES ARE "THE HOOK"

Just as you're unlikely to catch a fish without a hook, the same applies to readers. A subject line is the hook that can make or break an email pitch to a reporter or producer. Here's one that worked perfectly in placing an author-client on a YouTube show called *Best Book Network.* I pitched his book, *The Beer Diet*, as a fun, informative, sudsy read by colorful and witty beer connoisseur Gary Greenberg.

Here are the five words in the subject line that did the trick: "Looking for a sudsy story?"

Next came the first personalized line of the pitch, but remember: the recipient first had to open the email. "Bill, you won't find a foamier guy to interview than Gary Greenberg about his new book, *The Beer Diet.*"

Readers make split-second decisions on whether to open an email, and that decision is based on the all-important subject line, which should be crafted using action words that motivate opening the email. The best subject lines are forty to fifty characters, keeping it between four and six words. Emojis, coupon codes, humor, and creating a sense of urgency with a time-sensitive offer are other tactics marketers use to increase open rates.

Quotes are readers' keepers. No, not jeepers creepers, *readers' keepers.* Quotes can have a *gigantic* effect, making press-release writing not only much more readable but more engaging, believable, and impressive.

Here are two examples that show how adding quotes can make the release more inviting to read. And keep reading!

BEFORE

Anchors Aweigh Capital Hooks TransMedia Group to Introduce Its Newest Acquisitions in the Boat Industry: Century Boats and Club Yacht Charter

TransMedia Group has announced it has been hooked by Anchors Aweigh Capital, an investment banking and consulting firm in the maritime and industrial sectors headquartered in Fort Lauderdale with four additional offices throughout the United States, to introduce the recent acquisitions of American boatbuilding company Century Boats and Club Yacht Charter, a members-only club for chartering exclusive and luxurious yachts.

AFTER

Investment Banking Firm Sorfam Capital Ties up to TransMedia Group's Publicity Dock to Announce Boat Industry Acquisitions, Starting with Century Boats

Boca Raton, Florida—TransMedia Group takes aboard as a client the investment banking and financial consulting firm Sorfam Capital, for whom it will be announcing investments in the maritime and industrial sectors, including its recent acquisition of the ninety-year-old American boatbuilding company Century Boats.

TransMedia said it welcomes aboard one of the maritime industry's leading fundraising companies, Sorfam Capital, whose recent acquisitions of Century Boats will be making waves of news throughout the industry.

"Our publicity will underscore the depth of Sorfam's and Anchors Aweigh's experience in the industries they serve, along with their skipper's, Skip Sorenson's, many relationships in the boat, shipbuilding, and industrial businesses," said TransMedia CEO Tom Madden.

BEFORE

Famous children's book author Zane Carruth is bringing the tooth fairy right into your living room! Her new video series will consist of live readings for children and parents to enjoy from the comfort of their own homes

Carruth's books, "The World's First Tooth Fairy… Ever" and its sequel, "The Adventures of Abella and Her Magic Wand," will both be available in the upcoming video series readings.

The perfect series for you and your child, "a delightful book about adventure, bravery and how being curious is often a very good thing," said Zane Carruth.

AFTER

Tooth Fairy Book Reading Comes Home to Roost in At-Home Video Series for Children

Tooth Fairy stories by famous children's book author Zane Carruth will now fly off pages of her books and into living rooms as a new video series for children. The series consists of live readings for children and parents to enjoy from the comfort of their own homes.

Carruth's books—*The World's First Tooth Fairy . . . Ever* and its sequel, *The Adventures of Abella and Her Magic Wand*—will both be available in the upcoming video series readings.

The perfect series for you and your child. "A delightful book about adventure, bravery, and how being curious is often a very good thing," said Carruth.

BEFORE

TransMedia Group to Build Out Custom Public Relations Campaign with ShelfGenie of Fort Lauderdale a Franchise to Organize South Florida "Essential" Spaces

TransMedia Group (www.TransMediaGroup.com) will build out a custom public relations campaign for a new client, ShelfGenie of Fort Lauderdale, the top regional franchise that designs, builds and installs custom-made pull-out shelving solutions in essential spaces such as kitchens, bathrooms, pantries and more.

AFTER

TransMedia Group to Build Out Custom Public Relations for ShelfGenie, Showing How It Can Improve 'Essential' Kitchen Space in South Florida Homes

Boca Raton, Florida—TransMedia Group to present ShelfGenie's ideas for creating more attractive and functional kitchen space that has never been as important as today, with so many people sheltering at home and going so often to their kitchens during the coronavirus crisis.

Now just a brief word about hooks on those all-important parts of our emails, starting with this Q&A.

Question: what's the most captivating part of any email?

Answer: the subject line!

The Wordshine Man also polishes subject lines on emails until they succeed in arresting enough attention so the recipient will open and read them.

You don't open? You can't read! A subject line can make or break an email pitch to a reporter, producer, or potential customer.

You see, readers make split-second decisions on whether or not to open an email, and that decision is based on that all-important subject line, which should be crafted using action words that motivate opening the email.

The best subject lines are forty to fifty characters, keeping it between four and six words. Emojis, coupon codes, humor, and urgency created with a time-sensitive offer are other tactics that marketers can use to increase open rates.

Here's one that worked perfectly in placing an author-client on a YouTube show called *Best Book Network*. I pitched his book, *The Beer Diet*, as a fun, informative, sudsy read by colorful and witty beer connoisseur Gary Greenberg.

Here are the five words on the subject line that did the trick: "Looking for a sudsy story?" Next came the opening line of the pitch, but remember: the recipient first had to open the email.

"Bill, you won't find a foamier guy to interview than Gary Greenberg about his new book, *The Beer Diet*. Salud!"

We got Gary booked for the interview—or was it an inter-brew?

CHAPTER 5

LETTER WRITING ISN'T DEAD—IT JUST NEEDS A TRANSFUSION

Now, let's look at letters. We're going to see how letters from publicists to their associates, business partners, clients, and prospective clients can be catchier, more readable, and effective—sometimes just from some word changes or strengthening.

Please review the following "before" and "after" letters, starting with one letter warning someone not to make disparaging or slanderous comments or make potentially libelous statements about her or her firm following a disastrous conversation with an important third party she was attempting to refer.

BEFORE

> Carol, it's unfortunate that the lead I referred did not pan out, however, your mannerism has cost me a great major contact from your aggressive behavior and rude language telling a CEO to shit or get off the pot is not how I do business.
>
> That said, our reputation is extremely important to us as many judge by the people we do business with, that said I no longer wish to continue any additional referrals or relationship with you and do hereby put you on notice that I would not tolerate

any disparaging comments about me or my firm. Respectfully, I will do the same.

With that, good luck to you and your endeavors.

AFTER

Carol, it's unfortunate that the lead I referred to you did not pan out; however, your coarse language and insulting manner cost me that important business contact, who hung up during that call.

He hung up because he was repulsed by your aggressiveness and rude language. Telling a CEO to "shit or get off the pot" is not how to gain respect, win new business, or influence people.

That said, our reputation is extremely important to us, as many judge us by the company we keep and people we do business with or to whom we refer business. Therefore, I no longer wish to continue supplying any referrals or have any relationship with you, so consider our agreement terminated.

Under the advice of my attorney, I am hereby also putting you on notice that I would not tolerate any disparaging comments you might make about me or my firm, which has been doing business successfully for the past forty years. Respectfully, I will do the same in not saying anything disparaging about you.

BEFORE

Dear ______

The Honorable Jeffrey M. Perlow Chairmain of the Board American Friends of Meir Medical Center in Florida invite you to be part of celebrating the Third Gala Dinner by hosting with several hundred distinguished Jewish, community and business leaders from South Florida New York, and Philadelphia.

Joining us to pay tribute not only to Israel but also to our annual award-winners. Guest of Honor Senator Lindsey Graham. Graham is invite to receive an award from AFMMC.

Judge Jeanine Pirro, who will interview the Guest of Honor on-stage.

Event Moderator Mr. Freddie Roman Celrbrity Comedian.

The Gala Dinner will be held Sunday , January 26 evening 2020. At: Aventura Turnberry Jewish Center , 20400 Northeast 30th Avenue , Aventura, Florida 33180.

Meir Medical Center is an internationally recognized as one of Israel's most respected and strategically located hospitals, serving population of over a million from all faiths and with the highest percentage of pediatric patients of any other hospital in Israel.

AFTER

Dear ________

You are most cordially invited to consider sponsoring the American Friends of Meir Medical Center's Third Gala Dinner, Sunday, January 26, 2020, at the Aventura Turnberry Jewish Center in Aventura, Florida. This Gala will feature Judge

Jeanine Pirro interviewing Senator Lindsey Graham live on stage, plus other memorable moments.

By hosting this marvelous event, you'll be helping to bring a star-studded array of celebrities and important figures to a most distinguished audience of leaders in the Jewish community. You'll also be benefiting one of the world's great hospitals in Israel dedicated to safeguarding the health and welfare of over a million people of all faiths.

What a celebrity-studded evening it will be, not to mention what an awesome opportunity for you, your company or business, your club, or university to play an important, standout role in what will be "our biggest and best celebration yet," promises the Honorable Jeffrey M. Perlow, chairman of the board of AFMMC.

By sponsoring this great event, your name, your logo, your accomplishments will be in front of several hundred distinguished Jewish community and business leaders from South Florida, New York, and Philadelphia. So please join us in paying just tribute not only to Israel but to our annual award-winners, including guest of honor Senator Graham. The MC and event moderator will be celebrity comedian Freddie Roman.

As you know, Meir Medical Center is internationally recognized as one of Israel's most respected and strategically located hospitals, serving a huge population encompassing all faiths and with the highest percentage of pediatric patients of any other hospital in Israel.

CHAPTER 6

POLISHING DETAILS

It's essential to make details in news stand out, so shining them helps. Here are examples of key points in need of sprucing up, which sometimes can be accomplished through brevity.

BEFORE

> **CEO Briefing: Creating The New Marketplace . . . Water is The New Gold "Helping you Thrive in the World's Only Vital, Scarce and Recession-Proof Market."**

AFTER

> **Water! The New Gold Marketplace! A CEO Briefing You Mustn't Miss**

BEFORE

Healthcare Expert and U.S. Army Veteran Rob Snyder Joins Integrity Health Corporation

AFTER

Healthcare Expert, US Army Veteran Rob Snyder Brings to Integrity Health Corporation New Perspective on Disrupting Normalcy of Traditional Western Medicine

BEFORE

Sisco Corp-The Leader in Identity Management Solutions Unveils the FAST-PASS Contactless Solution

SISCO has created a Visitor Management Solution that will keep facilities compliant with the CDC's recommendations for mitigating the spread of COVID-19.

The FAST-PASS Contactless Solution eliminates the need to exchange materials between visitors and employees throughout the visitor registration process at a facility.

AFTER

The Leader in Identity Management Solutions, Sisco Corp, Unveils Touchless Registration for Entering Facilities in Compliance with CDC Recommendations for Mitigating Spread of COVID-19

Sisco Corp, the leader in identify management solutions, announced it has created a noncontact, touchless Visitor Management Solution to keep employees and visitors safe during registration at facilities in full compliance with the CDC's recommendations for mitigating the spread of COVID-19.

The new FAST-PASS Contactless Solution eliminates the need to exchange materials between visitors and entranceway employees throughout the visitor registration process at any facility, including boarding cruise ships.

BEFORE

Group to Rejuvenate Nourishing Biologicals' Media Exposure of Anti-aging Skin Care Products

TransMedia Group will now be overseeing all public relations interactions for bioscience company Nourishing Biologicals to promote their branded anti-aging skincare products.

To prove why Nourishing Biologicals has the most advanced skincare line on the market today, TransMedia Group will be contacting local and national media outlets focused on categories of health to schedule television appearances and print publication interviews.

"The Nourishing Biologicals team is very excited to begin working with TransMedia Group," Chief Medical Officer and CEO, Dr. George Sadowski, M.D., said.

AFTER

TransMedia Group to Rejuvenate Media Exposure for Nourishing Biologicals, Which Has the Most Advanced Antiaging Skin Care Products

To show why Nourishing Biologicals' skin care line is the most advanced, TransMedia Group will be scheduling television appearances and print interviews for the company's chief medical officer and CEO, Dr. George Sadowski, MD.

TransMedia said it will be overseeing all public relations activities for the bioscience company Nourishing Biologicals to promote its branded antiaging skin care products, considered the most advanced on the market today.

"The Nourishing Biologicals team is eagerly looking forward to working with TransMedia Group," said Dr. Sadowski.

"Our skin care solutions are crafted with natural ingredients, botanicals, and Nobel Prize-winning growth factor technology to treat your skin from the inside out."

BEFORE

Nourishing Biologicals' Dr. George Sadowski featured on Worldwide Business with Kathy Ireland

Nourishing Biologicals Chief Medical Officer and CEO, Dr. George Sadowski, M.D., appeared on the Fox Business and Bloomberg Television show 'Worldwide Business with Kathy Ireland' to share his company's products that are "exceeding expectations," according to Ireland herself.

"My focus has always been about helping people live their best and healthiest lives," Dr. Sadowski explained to 'Worldwide Business' correspondent Janna Burgess. "I'm so thrilled to have been given the opportunity to share Nourishing Biologicals on such a highly regarded program."

AFTER

Nourishing Biologicals' Dr. George Sadowski Tells *Worldwide Business with Kathy Ireland* Why The Company's Skin Care Line Is Most Advanced on the Market

Nourishing Biologicals' chief medical officer and CEO, Dr. George Sadowski, MD, appearing on the Fox Business and Bloomberg Television show *Worldwide Business with Kathy Ireland*, reports how his company's skin care products are "exceeding expectations," seconded by Ireland herself.

"My focus has always been about helping people live their best and healthiest lives," Dr. Sadowski explained to *Worldwide Business* correspondent Janna Burgess. "I'm so thrilled to have been given the opportunity to share Nourishing Biologicals on such a highly-regarded program."

With a background in bioscience, Dr. Sadowski discussed the formulas behind Nourishing Biologicals skin care products, all of which are pharmaceutical grade and sourced organically whenever possible.

Now, look at this one about a book signing. Why on Earth would your headline not mention the title of the book, especially if it's about Trump at a Trump event, no less?

BEFORE

Author to sign copies of new book At Tea For Trump this October

Peter Ticktin, author of 'What Makes Trump Tick: My Years with Donald Trump from New York Military Academy to the Present,' will be signing copies of his book at Tea For Trump on October 4.

"I am so thrilled to be signing my book at such a great event to celebrate my lifelong friend, President Donald Trump," Ticktin said. "There's no better place to share my story and I can't wait for everyone to read it."

With the event being hosted by Virginia Women for Trump at the Trump International Hotel to celebrate President Trump's belated June 14 birthday, Ticktin details in the book his experiences as the president's former platoon sergeant at New York Military Academy, available in paperback on October 27.

AFTER

Peter Ticktin to Sign Copies of His New Book, *What Makes Trump Tick*, at Tea for Trump in October

Peter Ticktin, the CEO of Ticktin Law Group and author of *What Makes Trump Tick: My Years with Donald Trump from New York Military Academy to the Present*, will be signing copies of his book at Tea for Trump in Washington, DC, on October 4.

"I am so thrilled to be signing my book at such a great event to celebrate my lifelong friend, President Donald Trump," Ticktin said. "There's no better place to share my story and I can't wait for everyone to read it."

With the event being hosted by the Virginia Women for Trump at the Trump International Hotel to celebrate President Trump's belated June 14 birthday, Ticktin details in the book his experiences as the president's former platoon sergeant at New York Military Academy. Available in paperback on October 27.

BEFORE

TransMedia Group to Grow Union Dental Holdings, Inc. ("UDHI") Public Visibility

TransMedia Group is eager to bring attention and grow public awareness to Union Dental Holdings, Inc. ("UDHI") by overseeing all media relations activities.

TransMedia to begin working on building UDHI's messaging, presence in the public sector, sending out press releases with looking forward statements and growing networking connections.

"The UDHI team chose TransMedia Group because of their sterling reputation with working with public companies" said Michael O'Shea , CEO and Director of UDHI. "I expect to be announcing great additions in the coming weeks that I am sure will give our shareholders the utmost confidence in the integrity and capabilities of our new UDHI team moving forward," added O'Shea.

AFTER

TransMedia Group to Open Wide Union Dental Holdings, Inc. (UDHI) Media Awareness

TransMedia Group to increase media exposure for Union Dental Holdings, Inc. (UDHI) by overseeing all its media relations.

TransMedia said it will build UDHI's messaging and presence in the public sector by sending out news releases illuminating its expanding networking connections.

"The UDHI team chose TransMedia Group because of its sterling reputation with working with public companies" said Michael O'Shea , CEO and director of UDHI. "I expect to be announcing great additions in the coming weeks that I'm sure will give our shareholders the utmost confidence in the integrity and capabilities of our new UDHI team moving forward."

TransMedia plans to launch a public relations campaign to help UDHI achieve its goals of gaining investor confidence while impressing NASDAQ that it's a public company to keep an eye on as it moves forward. "In the last month alone, UDHI has made great progress on all fronts, and it's only a matter of time until they begin executing their business plan impactfully," said TransMedia public relations manager Alana Pulver.

"When I met the UDHI team, I immediately saw their awesome potential for growth through media relations services we can deliver that will make them known and appreciated," said TransMedia Group president Adrienne Mazzone.

"Companies such as SISCO and Celsius Holdings Inc. (CELH) are two companies that we like to share as a case study, as their stock prices went up after we initiated our media campaigns to where the company praised and accredited it to our efforts," added Thomas J. Madden, CEO TransMedia Group.

By the way, UDHI has since changed its name to Xcelerate, Inc. (OTC: "XCRT").

BEFORE

Madden Talent Signs UFC Hall of Fame and WWF Legend Ken Shamrock to Its Roster.

Madden Talent Agency (www.MaddenTalent.com) said it will represent Ken Shamrock. Ken Shamrock is a UFC Hall of Famer and WWF Legend- Godfather of MMA.

Shamrock is a founding partner and brand ambassador for Valor Bare Knuckle, Inc. Shamrock is a 4x heavyweight world champion fighter known as one of the original bare-knuckle fighters in the earlier 'No-Holds-Barred 'era.

"I am excited to have signed with Madden Talent," said Ken Shamrock. "I am confident they are going to pursue the best business ventures for me and my fighting career."

"We are thrilled to have Ken Shamrock in our talent roster of professionals and feel that many opportunities are going to come knocking on our door," said Alana Pulver, Director of Talent Relations, MaddenTalent.com. Madden Talent is enthusiastic to represent Ken Shamrock in achieve goals from business partnerships to product sponsorships within the boxing industry.

AFTER

Madden Talent Signs UFC Hall of Fame and WWF Legend Ken Shamrock to Its Roster of Winning and Undefeated Talents

Madden Talent Agency (www.MaddenTalent.com) happily announced it will now be in boxing legend Ken Shamrock's corner as his hard-punching talent agent. Shamrock is a UFC hall of famer and WWF Legend—godfather of MMA.

Shamrock is a founding partner and brand ambassador for Valor Bare Knuckle, Inc. Shamrock is a four-time heavy-weight world champion fighter known as one of the original bare-knuckle fighters in the earlier No-Holds-Barred era.

"I'm excited to have signed with Madden Talent," said Ken Shamrock. "I'm confident they are going to pursue the best business ventures for me and my fighting career."

"We're thrilled to have Ken Shamrock on our talent roster of professionals, and we expect to be putting many opportunities into his corner," said Alana Pulver, director of talent relations.

Madden Talent is enthusiastic to represent Ken Shamrock in achieving goals from business partnerships to product sponsorships within the boxing industry.

BEFORE

TransMedia Group retained by iRecovery USA a Telemedicine That provides 'Assessment First'

TransMedia Group has been retained by iRecovery USA (iRecoveryUSA.com) to inform media on the groundbreaking advancements in patient care with Telemedicine in the addiction and mental health space. TransMedia will be sharing this upfront assessment approach via Telemedicine with iRecovery USA and their Dr's Melanie Rosenblatt and Dr. Jeffrey Huttman.

"The iRecovery team knew that groundbreaking is a very strong PR messaging that can be delivered by a reputable firm in healthcare such as TransMedia Group" said Dr. Jeffrey Zipper, CEO, iRcovery.com. "We've worked with them in the past on various projects and were pleased with results," added Dr. Zipper.

AFTER

TransMedia Group to Make iRecovery USA Known as the Leader in Advanced Telemedicine and First to Provide Assessment First

TransMedia Group said it can't wait to inform media about iRecovery USA (www.iRecoveryUSA.com), the leading recovery firm's groundbreaking advancements in patient care, with telemedicine in both the addiction and mental health space.

TransMedia will be sharing this upfront assessment approach via telemedicine with iRecovery USA and their doctors Melanie Rosenblatt and Jeffrey Huttman.

"The iRecovery team knew that groundbreaking is a very strong PR messaging that can be delivered by a reputable firm in healthcare, such as TransMedia Group," said Dr. Jeffrey Zipper, CEO, iRecovery.com. "We've worked with them in the past, and we were quite pleased with the results," added Dr. Zipper.

"Our ultimate goal is to create a collaborative care environment for our patients to feel safe and receive the treatment they need without disrupting their daily lives," said Dr. Huttman, iRecovery's chief clinical officer.

BEFORE

TransMedia Retained to do Publicity for Sleepy Eye Films' Chase Street

AFTER

TransMedia Group to Open Media Eyes to Sleepy Eye Films and Its Current Hot Project, *Chase Street*

BEFORE

Networking Guru Blanca Greenstein Unveils a New Radio Show 'Fired up with Blanca, Connecting in a Disconnected World'

Blanca Greenstein unveils her new radio show FIRED UP WITH BLANCA debuting on September 2 at 6:00 p.m. on 95.9 FM and 106.9 FM radio. The show shines a light on people of all ages who have overcome diversity and are thriving.

AFTER

Networking Guru Blanca Greenstein Unveils New Radio Show, *Fired Up with Blanca*, to Facilitate Connecting in a Disconnected World

Blanca Greenstein's new radio show, *Fired Up with Blanca*, debuts 6:00 p.m., September 2, on 95.9 FM and 106.9 FM radio. The show shines a light on people of all ages who have overcome adversity and are now thriving.

The show is the logical extension of Blanca's successful digital webcast, *The Laws of Life.* A former lawyer, Blanca realized that creating community and helping others become their best selves was more satisfying than practicing law.

"I have been to hell and back in my life, but I came back stronger. That's why I am fired up to interview guests that exemplify the fired-up philosophy of overcoming adversity. My goal is to inspire and ignite listeners to keep going, even when things get tough."

BEFORE

TransMedia Group to Shine Media Attention on Tiki Hut Livin's Stylish Sun Protective Apparel and Outdoor Products

TransMedia Group has been retained by Tiki Hut Livin and CEO Cheryl Capobianco in to deliver public relations expertise and media exposure strategies for the company's outdoor and ultraviolet protective apparel products.

On top of the other products being sold through Tiki Hut Livin's website, one product TransMedia said they will look to highlight is "The Tiki Hat," which is a fully designed women's hat that protects the skin from the harsh rays of the sun.

AFTER

TransMedia Group to Adorn Tikihutlivin with Stylish PR, Featuring Its Fashionable Sun-Protective Apparel and Outdoor Accessories, Starting with the Tiki Hat

TransMedia Group to accessorize Tikihutlivin and its stylish CEO, Cheryl Capobianco, with some fashionable media spin on its outdoor and ultraviolet-protective apparel, leading off with the Tiki Hat.

Among the stylish protective products featured on Tikihutlivin's website, one that TransMedia plans to highlight right off the top is the Tiki Hat, a fully designed women's hat that protects the skin from the harsh rays of the sun.

"We expect the Tiki Hat to blow the lid off the fashion world with such stylish protection where it's most needed," said TransMedia president, Adrienne Mazzone.

TransMedia will arrange media bookings for the company vivacious CEO Capobianco and send out press releases on her newly-designed products, along with other news about the company, keeping in mind how much outdoors lovers want to protect their skin from sun exposure.

"The Tikihutlivin team is so ecstatic to work with such a talented public relations firm as TransMedia Group," Capobianco said. "We want both men and women to be not only safe but fashionable too, and our products will make sure everyone still gets fun done in the sun.'"

TransMedia said it will present the Tiki Hat, along with eyewear, active wear, and gear to play pickleball to fashion and outdoor publications that will bring marketable opportunities to all of Tikihutlivin's products.

"We'll also embellish our messaging with stunning graphic design that will present Cheryl's prodigious creative talent to all those who wish to be fashionably protected," said Mazzone, an avid fashion lover herself.

"As soon as I saw the Tiki Hat, I knew I had to have one. Now I never go to the beach without it," said Mazzone, a Florida Sunshine State resident. "All of Cheryl's products will help you feel and look good staying fashionably protected."

BEFORE

iRecoveryUSA Telemedicine Addiction Answers Appoints Jeffrey Huttman as Chief Clinical Officer

Jefferey Huttman, Ph.D. is the Chief Clinical Officer for iRecoveryUSA.

Dr. Huttman oversees clinical care and is responsible for therapeutic programming, development, and areas of iRecoveryUSA's overall operations. In addition, he ensures that all of the company's programs maintain strict accreditation guidelines and consistently strive to reach the highest possible standards for outcomes and evidence-based care.

AFTER

iRecoveryUSA, a Leader in Providing Telemedicine Addiction Answers, Appoints Dr. Jeffrey Huttman Chief Clinical Officer

Jefferey Huttman, PhD, is the chief clinical officer for iRecoveryUSA, providing drug and alcohol treatment for persons with substance use disorders from the privacy of their homes.

1. Dr. Huttman oversees clinical care and is responsible for therapeutic programming, development, and overall operations of iRecoveryUSA, as it provides an affordable "whole-patient" approach to treating substance use disorders.
2. In addition, he ensures that all the company's programs maintain strict accreditation guidelines and consistently

strive to reach the highest possible standards for outcomes and evidenced-based care.

"It's an honor to be a part of such a brilliant and innovative team at iRecoveryUSA," Dr. Huttman said. "I'm very passionate about helping others who suffer from mental health and emotional difficulties, and our telemedical healthcare services are definitely the solution."

As a licensed clinical psychologist practicing in the field of substance abuse and mental health for over twenty years, Dr. Huttman is able to provide iRecoveryUSA's comprehensive and intuitive telemedicine to vulnerable Americans who struggle with alcohol and opioid dependency.

iRecoveryUSA's telehealth platform provides behavioral health services in a combination of individual video counseling, group therapy, and medication-assisted treatment twenty-four hours a day, seven days per week.

CHAPTER 7

THE PERFECT PITCH AND STORY WRITING

Public relations people are always trying to interest media in doing stories about their clients. In short, they're forever pitching to the press.

One of the principal tools to accomplishing publicity for clients is called the pitch. When you're in PR, you're on the pitcher's mound, constantly pitching story ideas to media, trying to pique their interest in doing stories. So you send them examples of the story, showing how newsworthy it is.

Here are some actual pitches before and after they were polished and an example of a story souped-up to make more publishing friendly.

MEDIA PITCH BEFORE

Dear XX:

How are you? Do hope this note finds you well! Wanted to reach out about a bombshell new book that shows President Trump's affinity for leadership at an early age as a potential guest for XX. We're more than happy to send you along an advance hard copy for you to review, should you be interested.

Are you familiar with Peter Ticktin? The South Florida-based attorney of The Ticktin Law Group released his first title through Mascot that explores his early relationship with Trump, titled *What Makes Trump Tick* as they both went to the New York Military Academy in their teens during the Cold Ware and saw the seeds of leadership coalescing already. In tandem with the launch of his book, Mr. Ticktin makes an excellent source to comment on the current political landscape, the upcoming November elections, ways on Keeping America Great and so much more.

We'd love to send you more info and happy to coordinate an interview with Mr. Ticktin, should you be interested in pursuing this further. his schedule is filling up fast, so please let us know as soon as possible.

As a starting point, enclosed below is his bio + book cover for you to review and the link to the book's official website. Looking forward to hearing back, thanks so much and talk soon.

MEDIA PITCH AFTER

Dear XX:

Upcoming is probably our nation's most important presidential election, so never has it been as timely to truly know the candidates and what makes them tick.

Recently there's been a spate of books casting President Trump as unfit for the highest office. Now comes a book about Donald

Trump when he was attending the New York Military Academy at age seventeen titled, *What Makes Trump Tick.*

It was written by someone who knows Trump perhaps better than anyone, as they were both teenagers learning to be military leaders. We would like to send you a copy so you can consider having the author, Peter Ticktin, on your show.

Today Peter is an accomplished attorney who has argued landmark cases. He's not only a fine writer but a captivating speaker who tells eloquently about his time with Trump and what they went through together as teenagers during the Cold War. It was then that the seeds of leadership were coalescing in young Donald, who was Ticktin's commanding officer.

Besides relating about his early experiences with Trump, Ticktin is an excellent source to explain why Trump is the way he is today as our president, and he can offer many insights on the current political landscape amid the upcoming November election.

We'd love to send you more info, and we'd be happy to coordinate an interview with Ticktin, which I'm sure your audience, left or right, will find fascinating.

Below is his bio and the book cover for you to review as well as a link to the book's official website: whatmakestrumptick.com. Also enclosed is a link to a recent video so you can see how effective Ticktin is on camera.

PITCHING PROSPECTS

Here are four examples of pitching prospective clients, trying to get their PR business. One is to an Italian named Massimo, called Max, whose wife owns a cosmetics company in Italy she wants to bring to the United States. He owns an Italian restaurant in Miami. The second pitch is trying to get Basanite Industries as a client. The company has a product called BasaFlex, an enhanced basalt rebar that won't rust like steel, but the company's marketing sure rusts, and its PR is nonexistent. It kills me to see something so marketable go to waste. As of publication of this book, I don't know if the pitch will win the day, but the prospect will lose out if they don't hire us to tell their story. We took the liberty of reserving the domain "Basanite Makes Infrastructure Sense."

We start with Max:

Hi Max, we love promoting cosmetics. We just put a skin care company on the media map called NB Natural (nourishingbiologicals.com). My daughter Adrienne, who is president of our public relations firm TransMedia Group, would love to talk to your wife about bringing her cosmetics here. We own a domain called BellissimaMax.com. Would she like it?

Also, I have a perfect product for your restaurant in Miami that in five minutes will sanitize it with UV light, eradicating any traces of the virus. It's called PleXus, and the owner, Dario Gristina, is from Italy, so you two will get along *ottimo*! We just placed an article in *Miami Community Newspapers* about how well it works.

CAPTURING A CLIENT

TM, this is TM, Tom Madden, CEO of the PR firm that's going to make your book a must-read by all those CEOs and other senior executives too busy to plan properly for the most important new position that's ahead—that of becoming the CEO of their own retirement. This will require them to direct three key divisions and putting all their acquired knowledge, managerial abilities, and talent into their health, wealth, and legacy. Too bad many think of retirement as the end of a career instead of the beginning of another one as the CEO of a major company called Retirement Inc., whose divisions are health, wealth, and legacy.

In his transformational new book, *Congratulations, You Have Been Promoted to CEO!: The Habits of Highly Effective CEOs that are Necessary for Retiring Healthy, Wealthy, and Fulfilled!*, Terry Mulhern has developed and chartered a course for CEOs to follow that will make them see retirement as another major business with three parts. They will be running as the CEO of their retirement—hardly the end, but the beginning of a stimulating new chapter in their lives.

Terry, we will all certainly read your book, and we thoroughly understand what you're offering. Since you seem to be seriously considering retaining us, I'll read it right away. I'm told you can arrange a discounted rate for us to purchase your book ASAP. But you know something? I believe we understand your three-part thesis already, at least enough that we could hit the core of what you're offering effectively enough to generate media interest. Let's have the media read your book. Review it. Write about it. Interview you!

So many authors come to us but won't hire us until we read their books. We're too busy to read every book that comes our way. I assure you that when you're a client not just me but everyone who works on your account will have read your book to fully understand its unique premise. Actually, I think we could throw out hooks right now to catch fish for you! Quicker you come aboard, the better!

WHY BASANITE NEEDS PR THAT WON'T RUST!

Basanite Industries needs one of world's top PR surgeons, Tom Madden, and his talented medical PR staff at TransMedia Group in its corner to lead an effective public relations campaign that will drive business to Basanite.

Madden and his team can prescribe the media medications and perform the operations the company needs to gain nationwide recognition at a time when, in a few months, the focus will shift from COVID-19 to restoring the health of our nation's infrastructure.

Basanite is in a unique position to do this, as it has developed the most powerful vaccine, BasaFlex, an enhanced Basalt Rebar engineered to add intrinsic value to a concrete structure and as a sustainable noncorrosive alternative to conventional steel reinforcement.

So to quickly rebound and prosper, Basanite needs to listen to the doctor who knows best after having saved and brought back to vigorous life many corporate patients—from AT&T to Kellogg's, from GL Homes to Illustrated Properties, and to the City of New York, for which it conducted an exemplary PR campaign for fair housing that won a Bronze Anvil Award from the Public Relations Society of America.

What good is having the vaccine ready to heal America's infrastructure if it's not widely known? And that's what TransMedia Group can do—make Basanite Industries widely known as a leader in noncorrosive building material that will keep America's infrastructure alive and well for many decades to come! That's why we'll say, "Basanite makes infrastructure sense!"

THE ATOMIC ANOMALY

The anomaly or something that deviates from normal or expected is a powerful tool in writing and a sure-fire way to bring readers aboard an article and anchor their attention. Here's an article about one industry the pandemic has actually helped to keep pleasurably afloat—boating!

IS THERE SOMETHING ABOUT RECREATIONAL BOATING THAT MAKES IT PANDEMIC-PROOF?

While popular venues and major marquee events succumb to the COVID-19 pandemic as we approach the fourth quarter, there's one recreational activity that has proven nearly invulnerable to the virus—recreational boating in both the United States and the global markets.

Be it for recreation or fishing within the maritime industry, boating is a timeless and popular outdoor experience that is persistently coveted highly by sportsmen and tourists alike.

Especially now during the current COVID-19 pandemic, there is a curious rise in the development and demand for recreational boating, so much so that the current market has skyrocketed, according to a recent published report by Global Recreational Boating in *MarketWatch*.

I believe recreational boating is a pandemic-proof activity that naturally lends itself to social distancing. Now, with the shuttering of major airport flights and travel restrictions, consumers are looking into other avenues within their own backyard to explore unexpected forms of personal enjoyment during these challenging times.

The health benefits that outdoor activities provide to people who want to get out, enjoy the sun, and practice safe social distancing all align with our newest acquisition, the classic American boatbuilding company Century Boats, known for its innovative designs in the center console arena.

This has spurred the rise of recreational boating in the Middle East and Africa as well, which can be attributed to the concentrated network of port cities and high-end and luxurious yachting. The shift and adaption to the current and challenging circumstance has led to a thriving market in the marine industry.

Boat shows this winter are anticipated to make a comeback after the mitigating challenges and decline in sales COVID-19 has brought on this past year. Directors are working to amalgamate their efforts to create a virtual platform that will act to support this upcoming year's boat shows. Most recently, up on the roster this month is the Jersey Shore Boat Sale and Expo this September from the twenty-fifth to the twenty-seventh. They are leading by example to respond effectively to the growing trend of recreational boating, and their actions are recognizable in the organization of an outdoor show that allows for a safe environment for consumers to shop and enjoy.

BEFORE

Nourishing Biological's Logic Line Treats 'Maskne' and Renews Scars From the Inside Out

Saint Augustine, Florida (November 3, 2020)—The most advanced skincare line on the market today, Nourishing Biologicals (nourishingbiologicals.com), has unveiled their Mask Logic and Scar Logic creams, now available for $14.99 each. Both of the Login Line creams have been reviewed and approved by professionals, as well as contain 100 percent natural ingredients.

AFTER

Nourishing Biological's Logic Line Treats Scars from Face Masks Called 'Maskne,' Improving Their Appearance from the Inside Out

Saint Augustine, Florida (November 3, 2020)—The most advanced skin care line on the market today, Nourishing Biologicals (nourishingbiologicals.com), has unveiled Mask Logic and Scar Logic creams, which improve the appearance of scars, including from face masks. Logic Line creams, available for $14.99 each, have been reviewed and approved by professionals and contain 100 percent-natural ingredients.

The following are just the leads without the headline.

BEFORE

The holiday season has finally arrived! The U.S. skin care brand NB Natural Powered by Nourishing Biologicals is running a seasonal sale just in time for you to prepare your gifts for a special someone. This year, the deals include a great discount on the brand's signature item as well as an option to bundle a few products with an extra discount.

AFTER

Naturally, the holiday season has arrived! And so can your advanced skin renewal come with it, naturally.

The US skin care brand NB Natural, Powered by Nourishing Biologicals, announces a seasonal sale just in time for you to prepare your gifts for a special someone. This year, the deals include a great discount on the brand's signature item as well as an option to bundle a few products with an extra discount.

BEFORE

World's Largest Organization Points of Light Honors President & CEO of FBS Properties, Fred Schneiderman

Fred Schneiderman, President and CEO behind NYC-based firm, FBS Properties, which has served as an investment platform for Oil & Gas, Real Estate and Private Equity Investments—has been awarded with Points of Light Honor.

The George H.W Bush Points of Light Honor Roll Award was created to recognize the efforts of everyday citizens from frontline to essential workers to those who are working in their neighborhoods and communities on social and economic justice and equity.

"Congratulations Fred, to be bestowed and recognized for this well-deserved honor and behalf of the such an incredible organization—Points of Light, said Jordan Jayson, Chairman/ CEO of US Energy Development Corp.

AFTER

George H. W. Bush's Points of Light Honors FBS Properties President and CEO Fred Schneiderman

Fred Schneiderman—president and CEO of NYC-based FBS Properties, a widely-recognized investment platform for oil and gas, real estate, and private equity investments—has made the George H. W. Bush Points of Light Honor Roll.

The Points of Light Award recognizes the efforts of everyday citizens, from frontline and essential workers to those working in their neighborhoods and communities on social and economic justice and equity.

"Congratulations, Fred, on being so deservingly honored by such an incredible organization as Points of Light," said Jordan Jayson, chairman and CEO of US Energy Development Corp.

BEFORE

Emergency Info Plan Joins Aventura Chamber of Commerce

Emergency Info Plan (www.emergencyinfoplan.com) is joining the Aventura Marketing Council/Chamber of Commerce (AOC) (www.aventuramarketingcouncil.com) to assist members in keeping their businesses safe. As a leader in creating accessible safety plans for every person, the Emergency Info Plan looks to help people feel safer during COVID-19.

AFTER

Emergency Info Plan to Keep Business Members of Aventura Chamber of Commerce Safe During Health Emergencies

Emergency info plan (www.emergencyinfoplan.com) to help business members of the Aventura Marketing Council and Chamber of Commerce (AOC) (www.aventuramarketingcouncil.com) to stay safe in health emergencies, especially during COVID-19.

I suggested to client that subheads are weak and to always keep punctuation inside quotes, especially in headlines. And being that local businesses are the biggest source of jobs, by providing this water-treatment option to local businesses, the company OriginClear Inc. will be helping our economy grow.

BEFORE

While Government Does "Big Infrastructure", OriginClear Focuses On Local Business Needs: "Water Systems In A Box" are designed for businesses that have to do their own water treatment

CLEARWATER, FLORIDA AND DALLAS, TEXAS—April 22, 2021—OriginClear Inc. (OTC Pink: OCLN), pioneering Water On Demand™, congratulated Florida today on its long-awaited grants to improve stormwater drainage, build seawalls and improve sewer lines, while it focuses on helping local businesses throughout the USA cope with their own expansion needs.

"The poor condition of America's 140,000-plus water systems is holding back local businesses that sometimes aren't even close to a sewage line," said Riggs Eckelberry, OriginClear CEO. "Our Modular Water Systems™ are mini-treatment systems designed for businesses that want to make clean water without going into the business."

AFTER

While Government Does "Big Infrastructure," OriginClear to Serve America's Biggest Source of Jobs, Local Businesses, with Efficient Way to Do Their Own Water Treatment

OriginClear Inc. (OTC Pink: OCLN), pioneering Water On Demand, congratulates Florida on its long-awaited grants to improve stormwater drainage, build seawalls, and improve sewer lines, while it focuses on helping local businesses throughout the USA cope with their own expansion needs.

"The poor condition of America's 140,000-plus water systems is holding back local businesses that sometimes aren't even close to a sewage line," said Riggs Eckelberry, OriginClear CEO. "Our Modular Water Systems we call "Water Systems in a Box" are minitreatment systems designed for businesses that want to make clean water without going into the water business, while concentrating on what they do best."

PIÈCE DE RÉSISTANCE

Here are two pitches: One is a GoFundMe for Bill, a prisoner who only had a few months left to serve on his sentence and needed money to get a fresh start when released. The other is a counteroffer to a TV producer who wanted to cast him in a TV series.

HELP REBUILD A LIFE: AFTER A DRACONIAN PRISON TERM, NONVIOLENT OFFENDER WILLIAM HAWLEY LAUNCHES GOFUNDME, VOWING TO FIGHT FOR PRISON REFORM

William Hawley has served over eighteen years in prison for a nonviolent offense. While serving his time, Hawley has evolved drastically and deeply repents for his past criminal actions. Hawley is due to be released from prison on February 24, 2021, after serving all that time for walking off a minimum custody work detail, a mistake he deeply regrets.

Do prisons ever reform anyone? The fact is, these horrible and dangerous medieval places often make convicts worse than when they arrived.

Yet occasionally someone rises above that wretched environment. They redeem and uplift themselves educationally, spiritually and emotionally.

They evolve from the dark Middle Ages of their past into a full-flowering Renaissance that is their future. And this happened to William Hawley, soon to be released after serving more than fifteen years for a nonviolent offense.

The reformed jewel thief and devout Christian will not only be trying to rebuild his life, but he'll be an advocate for prison reform while assisting other nonviolent offenders earn an honest living.

Bill has already done much good, risking his own safety and well-being to save several lives while incarcerated.

Most notably, he was instrumental in helping secure the release of two innocent individuals. In one case, Bill testified at a federal evidentiary hearing in Miami against corrupt, racist detectives who had beaten a false murder confession out of Tim Brown, a mentally-challenged Black sixteen-year-old, resulting in a life sentence. Partly as a result of Bill's testimony, Tim was freed.

While behind bars, Bill strove to improve himself. He loves to write. He became a published author and wrote a book, plus he writes countless letters to friends and supporters. Also, he excelled in courses from Washington and Lee University.

Despite his criminal past, Bill has always defended the weak and innocent against bullies. It's a theme that runs through his life as well as a memoir he penned about his experiences with Robert Durst, a multimillionaire and alleged serial killer now on a COVID-19 hiatus from his sensational trial for murdering his onetime friend Susan Berman. The book exposes Durst's evil deeds but is ultimately a call for justice for Durst's many alleged victims and their long-suffering families.

Bill wants to continue writing about his experiences, the characters he's met along the way, and his Christian faith. He'd like to speak to students and criminal justice and advocacy groups with an eye toward positive and equitable prison and sentencing reforms. Bill has in his corner public relations legend Tom Madden and is represented, pro bono, by the stellar attorneys Peter Ticktin and Francis Mota of the Ticktin Law Group.

Now fifty-five years old, Bill has lost everything he ever had and has been suffering through a living hell in a prison dominated by gangs and violence. It's sweltering hot in the summer and frigid in the winter, and now menaced by the spreading deadly threat of COVID-19.

Despite his ordeal, Bill has worked in prison law libraries, performs voluntary service on the offender representative committee, and serves as the medical department liaison between the offenders and the administration.

Through these activities, he has sought to improve conditions for all inmates. While previously serving as the liaison for both the chaplain's office and mental health department, he helped prevent the suicides of two prisoners.

Bill is not seeking a handout, but rather a hand-up in resuming his life and rebuilding his future. He will leave prison destitute, lacking the most basic things that many others take for granted: a car, computer, phone, and even clothing.

Still, Bill is willing to give back. Donations of fifty dollars will receive a free copy of Bill's book about his experiences with Robert Durst, which garners mostly five-star reviews on Amazon. Givers of one hundred dollars will receive not only a signed copy of Bill's book but a personal thank-you.

Help Bill to get back on his feet, and you will receive personal updates from Bill about his progress and everlasting gratitude. He wants those who support him to be his friends, to whom he'll always be grateful.

Now here is the counteroffer:

Dear _____,

I want to respond to the offer you made to William Hawley, who also goes by the pseudonym William Steel when he writes books like his *Sex and the Serial Killer: My Bizarre Times with Robert Durst*, destined to become a bestseller after its release, as we've not been able to promote the book properly since cameras weren't allowed in Durst's prison, causing us to have to cancel interviews with *Dateline* and other media who find Bill's life story intriguing.

First, let me introduce myself and the role I play. I'm Bill's close friend, publicist, and talent agent. I own TransMedia Group, a PR firm I started when I left NBC, where I was once upon a time the number-two executive at 30 Rock as vice president assistant to the president, reporting to my old boss, the TV wunderkind Fred Silverman, who sadly passed last year. I also own Madden Talent, a licensed talent agency.

For now, let me put on my agent hat in regard to your interest in and your offer to cast Bill in first episode of the TV production you're planning. So, in that regard, I'm acting here as Bill's agent. Having spoken to Bill, I'm sure you got a keen sense of how eighteen years in prison has not dulled his mind, body, or spirit one iota, and in fact, he's never been more creative, resourceful, energized, articulate, and expressive talking about all his adventures and misadventures in his former bizarre life so packed with them.

He's a different man now, totally reformed, but his memory of what he was and did before has remained clear as a bell, as he can relate in vivid detail the daring person he once was in the past.

Let's get right to the heart of the matter, which is always money. Bill wants very much to be in your production, but he feels what he brings is worth more than you're offering. Also, he brings me and my publicity capabilities and resources along with him, as I'm also his publicist who has a stake in his book sales.

Bill would be willing to accept $_______to be in the first episode, and he would like at least $______for each ensuing episode, with a 5 percent bump up for every one thereafter. Some of my services would come along with him at no extra charge. Of course, if you want a full-blown PR campaign continuing throughout, I'd be happy to discuss that with you.

Please let me know if you're willing to accept my client's counteroffer. I look forward to hearing from you. Call me direct on my cell.

—Tom Madden

Bill is now happy and enjoying his freedom in a small town in Indiana, where he's actually playing himself in a documentary being filmed there, which will be shown on a major network.

CHAPTER 8

PR CAMPAIGNS

Now we look at the Wordshine Man's writing aflame with passion, intended to incite action—in this case, to free an innocent Black American from a Texas prison. It's a bit lengthy, but try to stay with it, because so is Lamar Burk's prison sentence.

Burks has already served more than twenty years for a crime that newly-emerging evidence is strongly suggesting he didn't commit.

Still, a defiant defense attorney keeps her proverbial knee on his neck, holding him down so he can't breathe free air.

Here are highlights of the Wordshine Man's extensive PR campaign to free this man, now presumed innocent after so much new evidence has surfaced.

While he is still in prison, there are signs this campaign has won him much support, and there's even a film in production about him, plus many are now getting behind the Lamar Burks Defense Fund.

Below is an open letter to Harris County district attorney Kim Ogg.

IS LIFE IN PRISON ANOTHER KNEE ON AN INNOCENT BLACK MAN'S NECK UNTIL HE CAN'T BREATHE? OPEN LETTER TO HARRIS COUNTY DISTRICT ATTORNEY KIM OGG IN HOUSTON, TEXAS, FROM COURT OF PUBLIC OPINION ADVOCATE TOM MADDEN DEMANDING FREEDOM FOR LAMAR BURKS

Dear District Attorney Ogg,

You probably believe Lamar Burks is guilty of murder and deserving of his seventy-year prison sentence, of which he has served already twenty long, hard years, but with all due respect, you're *wrong*! He's innocent!

In light of new evidence that has emerged, could you apply a fresh perspective, considering that one of the two white DEA agents involved in this case against a innocent Black American man was himself convicted on seven counts of obstructing justice, perjury, falsifying government records, and other crimes?

Why has that agent's conviction resulted in overturning convictions of other felons he investigated, but not Burks? Is it because Burks is Black?

Wasn't Burks investigated by that same agent and his partner, who was also under criminal investigation? Did they not lie and coerce witnesses to testify against Burks?

What about Burks's claims that a wedding photo and call records prove his innocence? Why were the phone records not previously admitted into evidence? Also, haven't two witnesses recanted their stories placing him at the scene?

How do you respond to Burks's attorney, who says, "Mr. Burks was convicted based exclusively on false testimony, and it's disturbing how someone could be convicted for such a length of time based on faulty evidence."

Lamar Burks has served twenty years in prison for killing a man he didn't know. He's told the same story for twenty years—he couldn't have committed the crime, for at the time it occurred in Texas, he was en route to his sister's wedding in Louisiana.

Please consider that Burks was convicted largely on circumstantial evidence—no fingerprints, no verifiable proof he was at the crime scene, no DNA test evidence, and the lying testimony of a witness who later recanted.

Then another man steps forward saying he was the shooter, in addition to an underhanded investigation and testimony of two corrupt DNA agents whose bloody past for some reason you appear to be protecting. Some say you're now on a witch hunt, going after two former African American HPD officers. True?

Your actions are forcing Lamar to request continuances of his evidentiary hearing in hopes you'll release pertinent facts about one of the two DEA agents, Jack Schumacher. Perhaps your office could have investigated more thoroughly Lamar's assertions that he was in Louisiana when the crime occurred in Texas.

The other day, when your assistant called to berate me about a news release I had sent out, I asked him why your office never bothered to check Lamar's alibi placing him at a casino in Louisiana, so there's probably security camera evidence of his being there at the time of the killing during a late-night craps game behind a Houston club. But your agitated assistant said that Lamar should have done that. "That was for Burks to do," your assistant barked at me. Really?

Please consider this is now a different time when evidence of systemic racism is surfacing throughout law enforcement, and now, the pandemic is putting prison populations in acute danger, where they're packed in cellblocks like sardines.

Many of us firmly believe Lamar Burks is innocent. We've come to know this man. Trust him. We believe he was framed—set up by those two DEA agents. We exhort you to think about Lamar nonpolitically, in the clear light of a new day.

This man has already spent twenty years in prison. He has asthma, so he's a sitting duck for COVID-19.

If freed, Burks would not be a threat to anyone, as he is not a violent man, but just someone who wouldn't flip on an artist-client of his recording company, as those two DEA agents allegedly wanted him to do and then paid him back for refusing to cooperate.

Would it be a sign of weakness to have him released? Hardly.

It would show you to be merciful and wise, as new evidence is making the water what you've never wanted to see it become, muddy, thinking it would blur his conviction. But if this evidentiary downpour continues, it's only going to get muddier, blurrier.

So I urge you to give Lamar Burks a second chance instead of risking having an innocent man die in prison. Please remove the criminal justice system's knee, where it has been for the last twenty years on Lamar's neck. Let him out into free air so he can breathe

WHY WON'T HOUSTON POLICE CHIEF TELL HOW FORMER INDICTED HPD OFFICERS ARE LINKED TO 1997 MURDER CASE OF LAMAR BURKS?

Houston, Texas (July 16, 2020)—State lawmakers and civil rights leaders, sensing something fishy, have for months been demanding that Houston police chief Art Acevedo release an internal audit of the department's narcotics division following a botched raid at 7815 Harding Street.

One case that has yet to be reviewed in this same seamy context is the 1997 murder case of Lamar Burks.

Burks, who has already spent twenty years in prison, claims he was framed by rogue officers, and now new evidence shows that prior to the 1997 murder, he was charged by former officer Steven Bryant, who, while working undercover, made a failed attempt to tie Lamar Burks to a drug transaction involving three kilos of cocaine. Internal records and trial testimony reveal Bryant traveled with informants to Burks's recording studio seeking to purchase drugs, which was unsuccessful when Burks told him he sold music, not dope.

The effort to nail Burks did not stop there, for in 1997, Burks opened a nightclub in Houston's Fifth Ward, and a man named Derevin Whitaker, who had just been released from prison, approached Burks for a job at the club. Burks hired Whitaker, not knowing that Whitaker's aunt Bonnie was romantically involved with Officer Bryant, who, together with Goines, was attempting to build a case against Burks for the murder on June 30, 1997. At the time, evidence shows Burks actually was attending his sister's wedding in Louisiana when Whitaker allegedly shot and killed Earl Perry outside a Houston nightclub, for which Burks was later charged.

HARRIS COUNTY DA KIM OGG REFUSES TO RELEASE FACTS ABOUT EX-COP'S ALLEGED INVOLVEMENT IN SHOOTING DEATHS OF NINE AFRICAN AMERICANS

Houston, Texas (June 30, 2020)—More than nineteen months have passed since the formal request was made to the Harris County Conviction Integrity Unit for the release of the disciplinary file of former DEA agent John Jack Schumacher.

Schumacher, who was once investigated by Congress for civil rights violations, has been subpoenaed by state officials to testify in the wrongful conviction of case of Lamar Burks.

Burks has spent the last twenty years in prison for a murder he claims was pinned on him by Schumacher and partner Chad Scott in their effort to destroy black-owned businesses in the Fifth Ward Section of Houston, Texas. Scott was recently convicted by a Federal jury for lying under oath, falsifying records, falsely identifying suspects, excepting bribes, and stealing cash and other property during arrest.

Department of Justice has reopened this investigation into Schumacher's and Scott's involvement in the Burks case. On November 6, 2018, attorneys at Hughes, Arrell, and Kinchen LLP emailed and delivered a formal request to Harris County DA Kim Ogg and her Chief of the Conviction Integrity Unit Assistant District Attorney Gerald Doyle seeking the file on Schumacher.

Schumacher has been professionally disciplined nineteen times and who allegedly is responsible for the deaths of nine African American civilian while in the line of duty. The following exchange was captured on record between the late congressman Elijah Cummings and R. C. Gamble, chief inspector of the DEA, during hearings held on Capitol Hill, the House of Representatives Committee on Government Reform:

Mr. Cummings: "Did you look into Mr. Schumacher's background?"

Mr. Gamble: "Yes, I did."

Mr. Cummings: "What did you find?"

Mr. Gamble: "Disciplinary actions, that would be the only thing that I would be concerned with. While he was with the Houston

Police Department, there were nineteen allegations, complaints filed against him, and four since he has been at DEA."

Legal experts say that Lamar Burks's constitutional rights would be seriously violated if the Harris County DA's office continues to intentionally withhold what is known in legal circles as "Brady evidence." Without this evidence, lawyers for Mr. Burks would be denied the right to properly cross-examine Schumacher about his disciplinary history or subpoena as witnesses family members of the nine people Schumacher has killed.

The NAACP and Civil Rights Leaders have called on Harris County DA Kim Ogg to drop the charges. Any critics view this as blatant systemic racism due to Ogg's relentless pursuit of two African American former HPD officers. Burks's release the following statement:

"Ms. Ogg is engaged in a witch hunt of former HPD officers Gerald Goins and Stephen Bryant, two African Americans, and at the same time, she has given a pass to two white ex-cops who killed, tortured, and falsely imprisoned members of the African American community for over two decades."

Email to Lamar's daughter:

Fortunately, we got the release out before I received from the KPRC news director his denial of my request to insert the link to the KPRC confession interview into our new release. Still, I may be in a little trouble now—call it hot water—but it was worth it for your dad. Tom

From: Thomas Madden
Sent: Wednesday, October 23, 2019 4:52 p.m.
To: Strickland, Dave
Subject: Re: Lamar Burks

Thank you, Dave. Henceforth we'll respect your decision to remain neutral and objective in this case as a news organization should. I spent a good part of my career as a news reporter and as a television network executive, so I know the proprieties here, believe me.

Still, I commend your enterprising reporting on this matter. The fact that someone has admitted on camera in a televised news interview his doing the fatal shooting and stating my client wasn't even at the scene is itself pertinent, newsworthy and most timely with a hearing coming up on 10/29.

Therefore, I hope you will repeat this important interview as what all of us should be striving for is truth and justice. Thank you.

Tom Madden, CEO, TransMedia Group

On Oct 23, 2019, at 4:13 p.m., Strickland wrote: Thank you for your email. Unfortunately, I will have to deny your request. KPRC does not wish to be part of a PR campaign concerning our reporting. As a news organization, our reporting stands as broadcasted or published on the internet.

David T. Strickland

News Director, KPRC Television

LAMAR BURKS MURDER CONVICTION UNDER REVIEW AFTER MAN ADMITS ON-CAMERA HE WAS THE SHOOTER, NOT BURKS WHO WASN'T EVEN AT THE SCENE 22 YEARS AGO IN HOUSTON

Houston, Texas (October 23, 2019)—A DEA agent convicted of perjury and another man admitting on television he was the fatal shooter in 1997 has resulted in a new hearing on Oct. 29 for Lamar Burks. Burks has already served nineteen years in prison for the murder that new evidence is showing he did not commit.

TransMedia Group is representing Burks, as the PR firm's founder, Tom Madden, believes him to be innocent and also deserving of a hearing in the court of public opinion.

According to investigative reporting by KPRC reporter Brandon Walker, the conviction of a former Drug Enforcement Administration agent has raised new questions about the decades-old homicide case. Burks was convicted of murder in 2000 for the shooting death of Earl Perry.

Recent allegations of coercion, as well as newly-uncovered evidence, have Burks's murder conviction under review.

From: Thomas Madden
Sent: Wednesday, October 23, 2019 2:21 p.m.
To: Debbie Strauss KPRC
Subject: FW: PR Newswire Press Release Distribution for Lamar Burks.

Debbie and Brandon, please inform your higher-ups that this had to go out nationally a few minutes ago. With a most important hearing coming up, we couldn't wait. It had to go now. I'm sure your management would have approved, and I hope they'll understand and forgive me.

It's actually good PR for KPRC as you've been wonderfully enterprising on this story about an innocent man being framed and imprisoned for so many years for a crime he didn't commit.

(Picture of the Liberty Bell)

May It Ring Out Again for Freedom for Those Who Are Imprisoned like Lamar Burks in Houston

Q: What do Savannah, a Lake Charles casino, and a prisoner in Houston serving seventy years for a murder that new evidence is showing he didn't commit have in common?

A: Money!

That's because innocence has a price tag not everyone can afford.

Take the case of Lamar Burks who has a hearing scheduled Oct. 29 in Houston to consider a swath of new evidence that has emerged proving unequivocally once again his innocence.

Here's a guy who was playing poker in the Isle of Capri Casino in Lake Charles, Louisiana, on several nights while there for his sister's wedding June 29–30, 1997, at the time the murder occurred late one night in Houston, Texas.

There's video evidence of this, corroborated by records of phone calls Burks made from there on the night Earl Perry was shot to death in Houston on June 30, 1997, but at the time of his trial Burks couldn't afford to procure it and was convicted of murder.

Where does Savannah come in?

In 1733, General James Oglethorpe envisioned Savannah as a place where those freed from debtors' prison in England could get a fresh start in life. Oglethorpe named the thirteenth and final American colony Georgia after England's King George II. Savannah was its first city. Under the original charter, individuals in Savannah were free to worship as they pleased, and for a time rum, lawyers, and slavery were forbidden.

Today prisons in America for many like Lamar Burks are a kind of modern debtors' prisons, for at the time of his trial he couldn't afford to pay for evidence of his innocence.

WHAT IF YOU'RE IMPRISONED FOR MURDER BUT HAVE PROOF YOU'RE INNOCENT? IF YOU'RE LAMAR BURKS, YOU HIRE TRANSMEDIA GROUP TO REPRESENT YOU IN COURT OF PUBLIC OPINION

Boca Raton, Florida (September 27, 2019)—Currently serving a seventy-year prison sentence in Houston, Texas, for murder, Lamar Burks has retained the public relations firm TransMedia Group to retry his case in the court of public opinion based on new evidence that has emerged.

TELL ME THIS MAN'S A MURDER, AND I'VE GOT A BRIDGE I CAN SELL YOU

October 14, 2019

Hello, Houston, Texas—Here's witness subpoena list ex parte Lamar Burks case #08439680101C concerning our client whom we firmly—no, absolutely, incontestably—believe has spent nineteen years in prison here for a murder he could not have committed, as there's hard evidence he wasn't even in Texas when it happened.

Attached please find a list of material witnesses who will provide testimony and evidence to support Burks's claim of innocence raised in his active Writ of Habeas Corpus. Accompanying the witness list is a brief synopsis containing the relevancy of their testimony. Mr. Wynne, your last face-to-face visit with your client, Mr. Burks, as his lawyer was September 2, 2019 at the Harris County jail. We implore you to visit Burks soon as possible.

The purpose of this blog, which will be provided to all parties, including the presiding judge, the Harris County district clerk, and the court of criminal appeals, is to establish the applicant's due diligence to subpoena and secure witnesses during the evidentiary hearing here on October 29, 2019.

The witnesses and their proposed testimony are as follows: US Congresswoman Sheila Jackson Lee. She will provide testimony and documentary evidence related to the congressional hearing held December 6–7, 2000 in Washington, DC, and be highlighting federal, criminal, and civil rights violations by former DEA agent Jack Schumacher and Chad Scott, the chief architects of the murder indictment against Mr. Burks. Mr. Burks's murder conviction was the focal point during these congressional hearings.

(Many more witnesses are cited.)

Yes, it sure has taken a while, but finally, please Lord, at long last, let justice prevail! We have a great country, and our criminal justice system needs to reflect that greatness!

QUESTION: HOW COULD LAMAR BURKS HAVE BEEN CONVICTED OF MURDERING SOMEONE IN TEXAS WHILE HE WAS AT HIS SISTER'S WEDDING IN LOUISIANA?

October 7, 2019

This is one of many questions Lamar Burks has been struggling with while stuck in a Texas prison for past nineteen years for a murder new evidence is showing he could not possibly have committed.

An organization called the Innocence Project in Texas is beginning to wonder the same thing.

So many other pieces of evidence have emerged lately that are strongly suggesting—maybe screaming out is a more apt way of putting it—that he was wrongly imprisoned in Houston back in 2000 to serve a seventy–year sentence for murder.

I should divulge up front that my PR firm, TransMedia Group, is currently representing Mr. Burks in this matter, although we're charging him a much lower fee than we normally charge, as we're giving him an "innocence discount."

We give this special discount to any person or prisoner whom we believe is innocent and thereby unjustly charged or punished for a crime they clearly did not commit. There's also a slew of affidavits emerging like one from his older brother Scotty, saying Lamar was at their sister's wedding and was staying in Opelousas, Louisiana, with the whole family from June 29 to July 6, 1997, when the murder of Earl Perry occurred in Houston on June 30, 1997.

Also, documented phone records secured from AT&T show calls Lamar made from Louisiana during this time, which oddly were not even presented by Lamar's attorney at the time of Lamar's hearing.

Now more affidavits are coming to light by persons who witnessed the deadly shooting during a late-night dice game outside a Houston club. They're now recanting their earlier testimony that Lamar was the shooter and identifying another man as the murderer.

As if this weren't enough evidence of Lamar's innocence, there's new evidence that DEA agents allegedly framed him. One of them, Chad Scott, was convicted on August 27, 2019 on seven counts of falsifying government documents, witness tampering, and other crimes in an unrelated case.

The government now reportedly has expanded its investigation into Scott and his partner's activities in Burks's case.

A hearing scheduled on October 29 in Houston is expected to provide new insight into how Judge Denise Collins was a business partner of a DEA agent who allegedly forced an informant to implicate Burks.

This was apparently done as a way of getting incriminating evidence on an associate of Burks, Rap-A-Lot executive J. Prince, with whom Burks was discussing a distribution deal for Burks's hip-hop and R and B music company.

Letter to Mike Ware, head of the Innocence Project in Houston

Mike, with another hearing coming up October 29, we need to keep Lamar Burks's story and all the evidence emerging of his innocence in the public view, so I'm writing articles, blogging, and sending out news releases to keep the pressure on the system so maybe this time it will deliver justice for this poor guy.

Email to Scott Carruthers, managing partner, Ben Crump Law

Yea, Scott, it seems Wynne's not very active in this matter, which is why Lamar is betting on Ben. Lamar told me that he's not too fond of publicity, which make no sense.

From: Scott Carruthers

Sent: Wednesday, October 23, 2019 2:17 p.m.

To: Thomas Madden

Subject: Re: PR Newswire: Press Release Distribution Confirmation for Lamar Burks . ID#2620265-1-1

Thanks. I'll let Ben know.

Still have not been able to speak with Lamar's lawyer, Michael Wynne.

Posted on October 28, 2019 by maddenmischief

Now in Session

Burks's murder conviction is under review after another man admits on-camera he was the shooter, not Burks who wasn't even at the crime scene twenty-two years ago.

A DEA agent convicted of perjury and another man admitting on television he was the fatal shooter in 1997 has resulted in a new hearing on October 29 for Lamar Burks.

Burks has already served nineteen years in prison for the murder that new evidence is showing he did not commit.

According to investigative reporting by KPRC reporter Brandon Walker, the conviction of a former Drug Enforcement Administration agent has raised new questions about the decades-old homicide case.

At the center of the investigation were two DEA agents, Chad Scott and Jack Schumacher. A federal jury convicted Scott on seven counts in August. Scott is accused of perjury, obstruction of justice, and falsifying government records, among other allegations. The charges stem from Scott's work as a DEA agent in Louisiana after he was transferred out of the Houston area.

"Burks alleges Scott is guilty of the same in his case, and both Lewis and Brown now allege Scott coerced them into providing false statements," court documents said. An evidentiary hearing is scheduled on October 29 to consider new evidence showing Burks's innocence. The Lamar Burks Legal Defense Fund has been established to help meet the tremendous costs of legal representation.

Activists call for release of Lamar Burks.

The NAACP Houston Branch held a news conference Thursday, along with Burks's daughter and Ben Crump, a civil rights attorney, calling on Harris County district attorney Kim Ogg to drop charges.

LAMAR BURKS: IN JAIL EIGHTEEN YEARS FOR A MURDER HE DID NOT COMMIT

Federal agent is now charged with falsifying evidence in other cases; Burks's attorneys urge Harris County District Attorney to review case.

New evidence shows that former federal agent Chad Scott, now charged with falsifying evidence in numerous cases, played a critical role in the dubious prosecution of Lamar Burks, who is serving a seventy-year sentence for a murder his attorneys contend he did not commit.

Lamar Burks's murder conviction is under review after a man admits on camera that he was the shooter, not Burks, who wasn't even at the scene twenty-two years ago in Houston.

RE: Contact with the Harris County District Attorney's Office

Ms. Ogg, I called your office today to inquire about Lamar Burks's chances to be released, in light of recent evidence that has emerged pointing to his innocence.

I'm not a lawyer, but dealing with this matter as a former journalist who owns TransMedia Group, an international public relations firm. Attached is a recent blog I sent out summarizing what looks to us as compelling evidence of his innocence, which I'm sure you must be aware of.

I can assure you there's widespread and growing interest in his situation, and many in the media in and outside Texas are waiting to see what happens to him at his next hearing or hopefully beforehand.

If you would be kind enough to talk to me or email me a comment on this matter, I would be happy to share it. Thank you.

CHAPTER 9

REDEMPTIVE PR ON THE ROCKS WITH A SPLASH OF JUSTICE

C'mon, Crump. C'mon, truth. C'mon, justice. PR is rooting for you!

Vindicating and releasing Lamar from prison will be the biggest feather in PR's cap. And I'll happily offer a toast to justice with a double shot of Redemption Rye.

To whomever speaks pejoratively about PR—that is, *is this true or just PR*—I would say PR can perform nobly and be almost religiously redemptive when empowered by a shot of truth on the rocks with a splash of justice.

It can be the unequivocal key to unlocking facts, underlining new evidence, and empowering truth in a twenty-two-year-old murder case that is moving toward setting free an innocent man from prison in Houston, Texas.

I'm a PR guy who has promoted many things over the years, from Kellogg's Corn Flakes to AT&T cell phones, from fancy diets to delicatessens in Queens, New York, but never have I felt more proud of my PR because it is proving a man's innocence.

Hope is rising that Burks may soon be released after a flood of new evidence is showing a former federal agent now charged with falsifying evidence in numerous other cases may have played an insidious role in Burks's dubious prosecution.

Prominent civil rights attorney Ben Crump is taking on the more than two-decades-old case and held a press conference recently at the NAACP of Houston branch on behalf of Burks and his now twenty-one-year-old daughter.

His daughter told FOX 26 it's been hard growing up without her dad and talking to him over the phone between a glass window. She says her life goal is to free her dad, as a growing number of activists are also petitioning for his release from prison. Crump says he is working on an evidentiary hearing for Burks on January 22.

From: Reiss, Josh
Sent: Thursday, November 21, 2019 3:39 p.m.
Subject: RE: Contact with the Harris County District Attorney's Office

Mr. Madden:

Having carefully reviewed his claims for habeas corpus relief, the Harris County District Attorney's Office is confident in the integrity of Mr. Burks's conviction and sentence.

Cordially,
Josh Reiss

From: Thomas Madden
Sent: Thursday, November 21, 2019 1:35 p.m.
To: Reiss, Josh Subject:
Re: Contact with the Harris County District Attorney's Office

I sure would like to speak to you as I'm in Florida and won't be at the hearing next month while media are wondering about the DA's views on all the emerging new evidence of his innocence.

Was Lamar Burks not at his sister's wedding at the time? Were there not phone records proving this fact? Are the corrupt DEA agents who were involved in his case honest and straightforward in Lamar's prosecution?

Where are the on-camera confessions of another man that he and not Lamar was the fatal shooter that night relevant? Was the firing of attorney Andrew by the DA totally unrelated? Is the NAACP supporting Lamar's innocence meaningful? Relevant?

Even hypothetically, if he's guilty, is not serving nineteen years already not enough when there's mounting evidence he didn't do it? What if Lamar were to ask for nothing more than nineteen dollars if he were released? Would that help him?

I would love to hear the DA answer these questions and so would a growing number of media nationwide. Otherwise, it looks like a purposeful avoidance to deal with all this new evidence that has emerged. I'd be most grateful for a response as I'm a believer in justice and wish to see it delivered! Even if late. Thank you.

Tom Madden

On November 21, 2019, at 1:13 p.m., Reiss, Josh of the DA's office wrote:

Mr. Madden:

Your e-mails to the Harris County District Attorney's Office regarding your client Lamar Burks have been forwarded to me for a reply.

Having carefully reviewed his claims for habeas corpus relief, the Harris County District Attorney's Office is confident in the integrity of Mr. Burks's conviction and sentence.

I look forward to meeting you at the upcoming December status conference.

Have a happy and safe holiday.

Cordially,

JAR

I couldn't help but respond angrily to DA's representative: "Sorry, Josh, but that's a stock, right off-the-shelf, robotic reply that only creates more dissention and distrust of the criminal justice system, especially by minorities, many of whom are innocent yet are still convicted and imprisoned."

If your job is communications, I would advise district attorney Kim Ogg to communicate rather than stonewall. Take it from a communications pro like me—it's not a good policy to simply say over and over you have confidence in the integrity of a conviction when there is so much new and compelling evidence Burks is innocent.

It only arouses more distrust of the process that was administered by officials whose integrity is now in question, like those DEA agents who've been convicted of crimes in Louisiana. I truly believe the public will see it that way.

(For release 12/5/2019)

To: Harris County District Attorney Kim Ogg

Re: Beyond expressing your "confidence in the integrity of Mr. Burks's conviction and sentence," will you answer these questions tomorrow at his hearing?

Is it not true that the sole witness against Mr. Burks was a five-time convicted felon? Did you consider evidence including phone records and photographs showing Mr. Burks was at his sister's wedding hundreds of miles away at the time of the murder?

Was the corrupt and now criminally charged DEA agent involved in his case really being honest and straightforward in Lamar's prosecution? Are the on-camera confessions of another man that he and not Lamar was the fatal shooter that night relevant?

Was the firing of your attorney in Mr. Burks's case any way related? Is the NAACP supporting Lamar's innocence meaningful? Relevant? Even if hypothetically he were somehow guilty, is not having served nineteen years in prison already not enough when there's mounting evidence he didn't do it?

What if Lamar were to ask for nothing more than one dollar for every year he has spent unjustly in prison, a total of only nineteen dollars? Would that help you to recommend his release?

Why is it that despite all the new evidence that has emerged lately showing Lamar Burks could not possibly have committed the murder for which he has spent the last nineteen years in prison, all you do is keep repeating: "Having carefully reviewed his claims for habeas corpus relief, the Harris County district attorney's office is confident in the integrity of Mr. Burks's conviction and sentence."

Is it not possible at the hearing 9:00 a.m. tomorrow, you can answer these questions?

Respectfully,
Tom Madden, CEO

HARRIS COUNTY DISTRICT ATTORNEY KIM OGG'S SHUNNING OF CIVIL RIGHTS LEADER MAY COST HER REELECTION

Houston, Texas (December 5, 2019)—In a fiery yet heartbreaking press conference, Reverend James Dixon, VP of Houston chapter of the NAACP, alongside famed civil rights attorney Benjamin Crump, called on Harris County DA Kim Ogg to drop murder charges against Lamar Burks, who has been imprisoned for nineteen years.

Burks claims in his latest appeal that he was framed by ex-DEA agent Chad Scott. Scott himself was recently convicted by a federal jury on two counts of perjury, three counts of obstruction of justice, and two counts of falsifying government records. Scott also faces an additional trial in year 2020 on four additional counts and could face decades in prison. Witnesses in the Burks case have signed sworn statements stating Scott forced them to testify falsely before grand jury proceedings.

The sole witness prosecutors use during Burks's October 2000 trial was a four-time convicted felon who was a jailhouse informant working for Chad Scott. No other witness or physical evidence links Burks to the crime. Harris County DA Kim Ogg, a Democrat who ran on a platform of criminal justice reform, has yet to publicly address the NAACP or city leaders about the case.

Critics say should Kim Ogg, who relies heavily on the Black vote, continue to snub her nose at the NAACP, it may cripple her chances at reelection. Several democratic political strategists have viewed Ogg's silence as turning a blind eye to corruption and equated it to political suicide.

Email to Lamar's daughter, Jada:

Jada, tell your dad that Kevin Ratliff, the former Llano County police chief, is willing to testify on your dad's behalf and has only one tiny black mark against him: a misdemeanor for omitting something innocuous in a police record on some guy he thought was decent and deserved a break, but corrupt J. Schumacher was out to get him and trying to railroad him and set him up, as he's done to so many others, which Kevin can talk about, if subpoenaed.

Despite this one instance, I believe he's credible and certainly we should tease him without mentioning his name in my Monday blog that will circulate widely and certainly rattle Kim Ogg and draw media attention. Tom

Could This Be the Muddy Waters Kim Ogg's Worried About?

Houston, Texas—No, Your Honor, this isn't a song. It's a case about muddy waters of innocence versus injustice clear as a bell.

When DA Kim Ogg cites "muddy waters" in trying to block evidentiary hearings for Lamar Burks, she's not referring to the late blues giant whose vocals and piercing slide guitar we hear in Martin Scorsese movies like *Goodfellas.*

No, when Ogg uses the phrase "muddy waters," she's claiming a hearing for Burks to consider new evidence of his innocence would only, in her words, "muddy waters casting doubt on his conviction" twenty-two years ago, for which he's already served nineteen years in prison, all the while claiming he's innocent.

Lamar Burks Gets New Hearing in 1997 Murder Conviction after DEA Agent Lied in Other Cases

Houston, Texas—Lamar Burks, a man convicted of murder in 1997, will get a new hearing about his conviction in March KPRC learned Tuesday. Burks has always maintained his innocence, and the decision…

DA KIM OGG'S ASSISTANT GRILLED ME OVER THE PHONE YESTERDAY FOR A NEWS RELEASE THAT SAID LAW OFFICERS WHO FRAMED MY AFRICAN AMERICAN CLIENT ARE UNDER INVESTIGATION THEMSELVES

Harris County, Texas—Harris County DA Ogg's attorney phoned me, angrily citing what he called a serious inaccuracy in a news release I had sent out for my client, an African American who has spent twenty years in prison for a crime he swears he did not commit. And many believe him.

"What was wrong about the release?" I asked the DA's angry assistant.

"Did you not say in your release that the DEA agents who testified against him were currently under FBI investigation for federal, criminal, and civil rights violations?"

"Is that inaccurate?" I asked my incensed inquisitor.

"You used the word 'currently,' and that's inaccurate," he retorted.

When I told Lamar about this, he fired off this message to the DA's office: "Can you please refrain from sending threats to my PR Firm. All contents from my last press release are true and correct—see attached communication from US Attorney/FBI. Former agent Schumacher is currently under investigation. FYI additional press releases are coming, highlighting institutional racism by the Harris County District Attorney's Office."

Here was the headline in the release I had sent out:

HARRIS COUNTY DA KIM OGG PROMOTES WHITE PRIVILEGE FOR CONVICTED COP AND PARTNER INVESTIGATED IN THE DEATHS OF NINE BLACKS

Houston, Texas (June 10, 2020)—While the wave of riots and civil unrest has paralyzed every major city in America due to the death of George Floyd, a Black man murdered by a white policeman, Harris County DA Kim Ogg's policies protecting white criminal cops remain intact.

Now with the current "blacklash" and the African American community's uproar over the murder of George Floyd by a police officer, these failures may take center stage. Meanwhile, my client, prisoner Burks, says it's getting harder every year for him to breathe in prison with the district attorney's knee hypothetically on his neck.

TEXAS JUDGE ASKED TO HALT PROCEEDINTGS IN CASE AMID REPORTED BRIBERY ALLEGATIONS INSIDE HARRIS COUNTY DA'S OFFICE

Houston, Texas (June 16, 2020)—Fireworks irrupted inside a Houston courtroom on June 12, 2020 in a high-profile case involving a convicted ex-DEA agent and his former partner, once investigated in the shooting deaths of nine African Americans.

In a scene that could be compared to Curtis "50 Cent" Jackson's hit ABC series *For Life*, Lamar Burks, a former community activist and record producer, asked Judge Greg Glass of the 208th District Court to halt all future proceedings in his wrongful conviction case until the completion of a bribery investigation so that facts affecting his wrongful conviction case can be brought to light.

According to Burks, Radbil accepted five thousand dollars of an alleged ten-thousand-dollar-bribe on September 21, 2019 from an investigator licensed by the State of Texas and contracted to the Harris County district attorney's office. Upon further investigation, Burks found in an article published by Law360 that Radbil's license had been suspended by a federal judge in the northern district of Texas. Burks then contacted FBI special agent in charge Brian Ritchie, who in a series of phone calls with Burks tried to determine the source of the bribe.

Letter to House Representative

Dan,

At the suggestion of one of your constituent admirers in Houston, children's book author Zane Carson Carruth, the First Lady of Houston Rodeo, I want to bring a matter of egregious injustice to your attention, as it concerns an African American man who has been in prison for the past twenty years for a crime he didn't commit. If you can help persuade Harris County DA Kim Ogg to release information she has about two corrupt DEA agents who framed him, you'll be a hero.

And when you pass, you'll go right from the White House to heaven. Here's Zane's email to me suggesting I contact her fair-minded House Rep, yourself, regarding this matter.

"Did Misconduct by a Rogue DEA Agent Nicknamed 'White Devil' Result in a Wrongful Conviction in a Houston Homicide?"

Mike Hayes, June 22, 2020

Lamar Burks has maintained his innocence for nearly twenty-five years in a murder case that has been marked by conflicting eyewitness accounts and the conviction of a DEA agent on corruption charges.

In 2019, the Harris County District Court granted Burks a review of his murder conviction. Later that year, a Drug Enforcement Administration agent who investigated him was convicted in federal court on a slew of corruption charges.

After some delays, a hearing was scheduled for April but later postponed. Meanwhile, Burks remains in the Harris County jail—which has been called a COVID-19 "ticking time bomb." There have been more than 1,000 COVID-19 cases connected to the jail.

CONCLUSION

Well, the moral of this lengthy, grizzly, inconclusive chapter, which I want preserved on the record in this book, is that the criminal justice system sometimes moves like a snail.

Maybe a pregnant sea turtle is a more apt description, as the thousand of unborn babies she's dragging across the COVID -19- hot sand weighing her down and slowing her progress are those poor, innocent souls suffering in prisons like Lamar.

So, besides effective writing, it may take a one-hundred-thousand-piece orchestra and chorus to get a sliver of the system's attention plus a hundred baritones and sopranos to breathe some life and purpose into it, in an aria called "Justice for All!", conducted by the Wordshine Man.

But let me not end such a distressing and appalling situation as an innocent man buried alive in a dark prison by a heartless DA who seems intent on locking up people and throwing the key away.

Let me close with some samples of my favorite types of writing.

CHAPTER 10

HUMOR AND SATIRE

First off, I'll share my startling new pandemic vocabulary.

There is so much newness and blueness in our lives these pandemonic days that it might not only be appropriate but necessary to consider expanding our vocabulary.

Here are some new terms that will take us into the far reaches of this pandemic as we hide from the wicked witch virus from China, from which sadly too many of us are dying as we await vaccines that were supposed to come at warp speed yet move more like warped molasses toward starving arms.

Let's start with the following:

encyclopandemia. A definitive work unraveling information on pandemics, particularly focused on knowledge comprehensively derived from and concerning China's not-so-subtle coronavirus or COVID-19 invasion of the United States and the rest of the world in 2020.

stimulati. Meager, barely stimulating handouts from a torturously slow-moving government to a desperate populace, providing people with just enough to live on and stay relatively tranquil during a pandemic so there will be no uprisings.

lockdownagens. A strategy bordering on demented depravity designed to diminish enterprise and will to work by ordering businesses to close and populations to stay at home, leaving the masses dulled, powerless, and stupefied and all decisions left in the hands of those in power proclaiming they know better.

dissidents demasked. This is an immunity careless herd of idiots stampeding shoulder to shoulder, congregating in bars, restaurants and at wild at-home, face mask defrocked parties, tossing social distance to the winds and adamantly avoiding washing their hands.

Vaccinophiles. Wannabe celebrities, including mediocre senators, taking a shot in the arm to win one for the Gipper. They barge into the same spotlight as President Biden and Dr. Fauci, volunteering to be injected with a vaccine protecting against COVID-19, and hopefully its many new faster walk-in strains now surging, plaguing the world with a more contagious form of its original slower-spreading viral ancestor.

Cuomophobia. Fanatically overreacting and taking excessive precautions to escape from a presumed imminent threat of a pervasive pestilence spreading its horrific wings, about to devour an entire city already reeling from lockdowns, quarantines, and lost business.

Trumpophile. Intense supporter of President Donald J. Trump, who did practically anything to keep himself in office, even if having to act—pardon the expression—civil.

Trumpertantrums. Firing off flurries of tweets attacking critics, especially Democrats, presumed to defy reason, logic, and common decency when counting votes.

Bidentures. Removable plates or frames holding one or more artificial political planks designed to appease the liberal wing without upsetting Republicans too much.

Bidentistry. Filling cavities left by a political adversary and predecessor who once called you "sleepy" until you woke him up and shook him out of bed.

Think about adding these new terms to your vocabulary, and while you're mulling it over, please stay guarded, unassailable, and that four-letter word—safe!

Here's what I wrote in my blog, *Madden Mischief*, about my condo stopping a necessary but noisy balcony restoration project because it was bothering the snowbirds, so they put it off until after the part-time residents returned home.

They're called snowbirds because they flee the winter snow up north and come down to Florida just for the winter.

It's unfair to us year-round residents to halt projects just for their benefit for they are the condostocracy.

ROYALTY

KINGS, CONDO PRESIDENTS, AND SNOWBIRDS ARE THE PRIVILEGED FEW IN FLORIDA

Know ye this immutable fact. The all-powerful rulers in Florida are a privileged, high-and-mighty class called the condostocracy.

All societies, countries, communities, corporations, and Florida condominiums have the same basic structure.

First there are the aristocrats, the privileged few comprising dictators, elder statesmen, governors, CEOs, Fed chairmen, and the condo kings and queens with the title "condo president."

They rule along with dukes and duchesses, the part-time condo residents called snowbirds.

The latter are royals returning to their warm, sunny condos from northeast castles now freezing cold as winter sets in. They're an important part of the condo aristocracy.

Then there are the plebeians, the rank and file commonly referred to as the herd of year-round condo residents who fall into the vast middleclass of ordinary citizens, taxpayers, first responders, working stiffs and retirees whom you'll find ghost walking on beaches and golf courses or zombielike in their condo swimming pools.

Lastly and sadly, there are the underprivileged, the poor downtrodden condoless masses stuck at the bottom of the residential ladder.

They're either renting overpriced apartments or serving time in mortgaged homes with one and two-car garages in heavily fortified gated communities, miles from the ocean. They are stuck there because they see oceanfront condos as beguiling mousetraps that catch their prey by fooling them into thinking the cream cheese is free on Bagel Wednesdays.

Bobbling up and down all three levels are the artists, actors, musicians, and writers like myself.

I was president of a condo once, so help me, and wrote a satiric get-even book about it titled *King of the Condo*. Now I'm just a common condo resident, a perennial beach walker and blogger who runs his PR firm remotely.

Now I'll tell you why I'm writing this.

Last week there was a vote to stop the noisy but needed balcony restoration.

Why?

It was decided to do so out of respect for and in deference to the privileged snowbirds now returning from their palatial northeast nests. They like it nice and quiet while they're here.

We who are in that middle-class category of year-round residents can deal with the noise when it starts again after the privileged snowbirds depart in summer.

After all, they are the almighty snowbirds, and I guess we're just the year-round jailbirds.

Oh, it was done democratically all right, by vote, of course, though a majority of the residents are snowbirds.

I'm going to look into starting a condominium electoral college.

This way, if we should lose the popular vote, maybe we could still win and the noise and disruption can be spread more evenly among full-time and part-time residents.

Also, I'm suspicious of how the voting was handled, so I may be talking to Rudy Giuliani about it. Today you just can't trust elections! Power to the plebeians, the year-round condo residents. We dislike noise as much as the elites but just want it spread evenly.

Now, here are the pieces of satire aimed at a most serious subject: the 2020 presidential election.

Yes, it became steeped and embroiled in controversy, baseless charges, absurd accusations, lawsuits without merit, and grandiose declarations by Trump that he won and was reelected to a second term.

I equated it all to horse racing, calling it the America Derby and giving it a prophetic last line that summed it all up.

CHAUVINISM

Did you know the last name of former Minneapolis police officer Derek Chauvin has long been in ill repute in dictionaries worldwide?

The word *chauvinism* is typically used in the senses of either "an attitude of superiority toward members of the opposite sex," or "undue partiality or attachment to a group or place to which one belongs, has belonged, or maybe to which one has been assigned"—perhaps a police precinct?

The word may now have a sad new wrinkle and stretched to also mean an attitude of superiority toward another's race or ethnicity that is different from one's own.

As we all know, Chauvin was just convicted of murdering George Floyd, which infuriated millions and set off angry protests in the Twin Cities and around the world.

According to *Merriam-Webster*, "*Chauvinism* came into English from the French *chauvinisme*, taken from the name of a character (Nicolas Chauvin) in Théodore and Hippolyte Cogniard's 1831 play *La Cocarde tricolore.*

"Chauvin was noted for his excessive devotion to duty and patriotism, and this character trait is strongly reflected in the earliest recorded sense of *chauvinism* ("excessive or blind patriotism").

"The earliest known use was in 1851, but recent findings show we've been chauvinistic since at least the beginning of the 1840s."

LAST NEW WORD OF THE DAY—"PELOTON"

(Published 5/9/21 CommPRO.biz)

New Word Enters Crisis Management Vocabulary: Don't "Peloton" Me, Pal, Do a Recall!

When you have a product that kills someone, don't just "peloton," do something! In other words, don't just apologize, take action so it won't happen again.

Thus, it seems a new word has entered the PR crisis management lexicon.

Perhaps "don't peloton" will now join phrases like "stop Boeing a dead horse." Stop blaming others. Do something yourself to make sure it doesn't happen again!

This, of course, is a reference to how another high-flying company seemed to strongly intimate that the deadly 737 Max crashes were much more the pilot's than their plane's fault. So when you have product that's responsible for a child's death, you need to do sooner what Peloton has finally done after seemingly frozen for weeks in the headlights of the House consumer protection subcommittee's chair urging the company to recall its treadmills.

First thing we learned in crisis management is to take responsibility, then take actions to see it never happens again. We're supposed to apologize if someone is hurt or killed using one of our products, then take immediate steps to make sure the problem or flaw is fixed, whether it involves emergency repairs or a full recall.

While it took too long, the good news from a PR standpoint is that Peloton apologized on May 5 for failing to act promptly after reports that its treadmills are potentially dangerous. Eventually, the company recalled them and will now halt sales of one treadmill model linked to the death of a six-year-old.

The bad news is Peloton took weeks before it acted decisively after it had stubbornly ignored calls for a recall from politicians, federal regulators, and others. Peloton's botched response may go down as another egregious example of how not to deal with a crisis.

The question for Peloton now is how much this scandalous episode will dent the reputation of its main business, exercise bicycles, the demand for which has soared during the pandemic along with its stock price, now backtracking a bit.

As the pandemic abates, all businesses now will be heading back out into deeper waters with more valuable assets aboard, so it's essential they keep an experienced PR firm at their side 24/7. This is not only to keep media informed and excited about new developments and progress but to manage any crisis that might come up along the way as the company grows.

Now here are articles and blogs on subjects bothering me at the time, at which I had to fire my prose like a pistol aimed at different annoyances.

ARMS ON THE BATTLEFIELD

Like so many Americans these days, we've become veritable pincushions.

First it was the flu shot in my arm to thwart the latest influenza.

Then came vaccinations one and two to ward off the creepy crawling Charles Manson–like COVID-19.

Yesterday I took another needle for pneumococcal pneumonia, and again my brave arm is wounded and sore from this injection battlefield.

Next my battle-weary doc wants me vaccinated for shingles, which he said won't kill me but would torment me with a painful rash causing pins and needles. More needles!

Then I'm to take a tetanus shot, as he warned that's another killer on the loose we must ban from our bodies now targeted by so many ruthless enemies.

This morning my brave, undaunted foxhole wife, Rita, was my emergency medic. She tweezed a tiny spec of glass out from under my big right toe that had been pinching me all night. Probably I had picked up the sneaky, prickly lodger from one of our daily beach patrols.

Yes, these days Rita and I are like sentries on guard. Whenever suspicious pedestrians approach us, we pop on our face masks and circle around them suspiciously.

Yes, we're at war!

It's not pretty. It's painful. And the only arms we have to fight with are our arms!

I can't wait for that armistice.

There are so many other things we could be doing for armusement!

THE AMERICA DERBY: HOW WE PICK LEADERS IS MORE LIKE BETTING ON HORSES AT PIMLICO

December 14, 2020

The contenders in this past America Derby were the favorites, "the Economy" (3 to 2) ridden by Donald Trump and "Pandemic" ridden by Joe Biden (2 to 1).

Pandemic is the only horse with blinders while—besides the conventional hat and goggles—jockey Biden proudly dons his signature face mask.

Many horse race handicappers say if Trump wasn't such a stubborn jockey, he could easily win if he wore a face mask too and kept distance from fans who made him a heavy favorite.

Other horses in this year's America Derby were "Systematic Racism" (4 to 1), "Immigration" (10 to 1), "Juris Prudence" (6 to 1), "Supreme Court" (7 to 2), "Healthcare" (6 to 2), "Climate Change"

(20 to 1), "Criminal Justice" (5 to 1), "Coronavirus Vaccine" (30 to 1), "Higher Taxes" (20 to 1), "Obamacare" (20 to 1), and "Tariff Diplomacy" (20 to 1).

They're off!

Health Care takes the lead followed by Supreme Court second, Obama Care third. Then Juris Prudence, Climate Change, and Criminal Justice.

As they turn into the backstretch, coming up fast on the outside is Systematic Racism taking second place, Obama Care drops to third, with Health Care still in front by a furlong as we head into the homestretch.

Now Juris Prudence and Coronavirus Vaccine make their moves racing up to third and fourth place followed by Immigration, Tariff Diplomacy, then Supreme Court, the Economy, and Pandemic.

Now heading into the homestretch, picking up speed the Economy moves up to third place with Pandemic a close second as the two are almost neck and neck heading to overtake the leader Health Care.

It's a battle in the stretch with Pandemic and the Economy, edging by Health Care, and racing neck and neck. They cross the finish line.

It's Pandemic by a nose!

The winner is Pandemic, but wait a minute, there's a flag, an objection, so maybe Pandemic is not the winner, as one of the judges says there was a foul committed against the Economy. Something to do with mail-in ballots.

We'll have to see what happens after judges watch the film to decide if a foul was indeed committed.

Yes, ladies and gentlemen, the judges have ruled that the finish stands. Pandemic is the winner. And it's just as the handicappers called it.

If there was no Pandemic, the Economy would have won!

I'M A DOMESTIC ONE-HOOFED HUSBAND ANXIOUSLY AWAITING HERD IMMUNITY

December 21, 2020

Hello. Can you tell me where the herd is? I'd like to join it, the one with the immunity everyone's talking about. I need it bad!

I've been waiting impatiently cloistered in my condo pasture, while immunity is taking its sweet time to come home to me. Meanwhile, I see no sign of any herds in the bleak offing.

Yes, I'm seeing others being vaccinated on TV, which is encouraging, and a hopeful sign. Yet the media keep drumbeating the deaths spiraling upward, out of control each day, and it's making me more nervous by the minute.

When she sees the Pfizer needles zoom into nurses' arms on TV, my wife, Rita, turns her head away, as it makes her almost nauseous. Not me! I'd take the shot right in my snout and smile just like Elvis did when he got his famous polio shot, if that would make my vaccination come sooner. I'm itching for that damn needle.

You see, I'm over sixty-five. I'm a domestic one-hoofed husband who's a sitting duck for COVID-19. Right, Dr. Fauci? You tell 'em!

So I'm staying home in my condo stable, yearning to run with the pack, that illusive herd of immunity. In the meantime, I'm well-armed with my trusty, fully-loaded PleXus zapping the "COVID kid" wherever he may be lurking in my apartment.

Quick on the draw, I shoot him dead with my UV-650 I call E PleXus Unum, for out of many rays, it's one killer device protecting my ass.

Still, I want to join that herd. That's the safest solution. I don't care if it's a herd of cows. I'll go with the flow, even though I don't think Rita would appreciate my running around with fully-grown females of any species.

I'll assure her that I'll still wear my face mask, stay socially distant, and religiously faithful.

Isn't that right, Dr. Gupta? Even immune, you can still spread it.

WILL THERE BE ENOUGH DIVERSITY IN THAT WHITE IGLOO IN WASHINGTON?

December 28, 2020

I don't know about you, but I'm 90 percent satisfied with Joe Biden's "most diverse" cabinet in history.

I just hope we continue to fill cabinet positions with people who are not just diverse but supersmart, fully capable.

Yes, certainly the president-elect has taken steps in the right diverse direction. No question. And his choices seem bright enough and the diversity will surely shatter stereotypes and batter bias when we see it performing in our country's best interest. Bravo, Biden.

Like Biden, I'm a firm believer in diversity, but I think he's playing just a wee bit too safely between the ten- and twenty-yard line without scoring diversity touchdowns.

Yes, there's a finally a Native American onboard. My friend Silverbird is happy about that.

He opened one of the first Native American restaurants in Manhattan, serving delicious snakes. I gave him the name for his place, his own—Silverbird.

And there's the first gay secretary of transportation. I have a daughter who's happy about that.

And for the first time since Obama, my Black buddies will have something to high-five about with our incoming Secretary of Defense.

But why isn't there someone really ethnic? How about an Inuit?

Look at what they have endured. Surely one can serve as a model of coping with lockdowns and harsh climates as a member of that most diverse cabinet in history.

And how about a native Hawaiian? Wouldn't that make the racial and ethnic diversity stand out?

Our fiftieth state is the only one outside North America, the only island state, and the only state in the tropics. Chinese, Japanese, Korean, Thai, and Filipino immigrants whose ancestors once worked on the island's sugar cane and pineapple fields are collectively the largest group on the island.

And why isn't there a Chinese American citizen from one of the thriving Chinatowns across America? Now that might even endear China's President Xi Jinping to the Biden diversity.

And what about the many homeless? Why can't they be represented too? Why not a cabinet post established for someone from that downtrodden community? Couldn't we learn better how to help the homeless by having a representative of that community in the cabinet?

Next, let's look to Appalachia, to Kentucky coal miners, and to the bayous of Louisiana to stretch diversity out even further.

But let's just keep in mind that while diversity is wonderful we still need talented, experienced people running our government.

PLEASE PARDON THIS PARODY ON PARDONING

January 4, 2021

First, if you don't mind, I would like to add a few pardons of my own.

I want to pardon my daughter for giving me so many nuts for Christmas.

They were in this humongous bag stuffed in a large wicker basket wedged between two odd-couple bottles, one containing rubbing alcohol, the other my favorite vodka. Thanks Adrienne, I'll be cracking, rubbing and chugging all year long! But it was the thought for which I thank you.

Next, I would pardon Roger Stone for wearing those ties, tight vests, and jackets, capped by that black fedora top hat and dark glasses like he just came strutting out of a gentlemen's parlor during the roaring twenties.

Then I hasten to congratulate my esteemed client Peter Ticktin, who was the lawyer who presented the petition to President Trump to pardon Boca Raton, Florida, real estate mogul James Batmasian.

The crime to which Batmasian had pled guilty involved a technical tax evasion matter, while he does much to help homeless and other charities.

Coincidentally, Ticktin wrote the latest and probably most favorable book about Trump, *What Makes Trump Tick: My Years with Donald Trump from New York Military Academy to the Present.*

Then I would pardon President Trump himself for overpardoning all his cronies like Stone. While left-leaning media clocks him exceeding the pardon limit in his waning days in the White Igloo, conservative media pardon him for not wearing his face mask at those jam-packed rallies that looked great on TV but were perhaps as much virus-spreaders as vote-getters.

Next, on a more somber side, I would pardon my Black friend Lamar, who has already spent over twenty years in prison for fatally shooting someone during an early morning dice game outside a Houston nightclub.

Lamar Burks must have been one hell of a craps shooter, for at the time evidence shows he was at his sister's wedding in Louisiana. Still, Houston DA Kim Ogg refuses to take her proverbial knee off poor Lamar's neck, so he's near forgetting what it's like to breathe free air—poor guy.

I also would pardon another prisoner, William Hawley, who wrote a book about an alleged "serial killer," the billionaire Robert Durst, which I subtitled *Dursturbed.*

My PR firm, TransMedia Group just set up "Help Rebuild a Life," a GoFundMe account for Bill, so that when he's finally released on February 24, after serving a draconian eighteen-year sentence for nonviolent offenses, he can devote what's left of his life to raising awareness of the need for prison reform.

While serving his time in Virginia, Hawley has evolved drastically and deeply repents his past criminal actions in Florida, where he was convicted.

He spent a big chunk of that prison time for walking off a minimum custody work detail, a mistake he deeply regrets. During his time behind bars, Hawley has become a devout Christian, a skilled writer, an academic, and an advocate for justice. I pray that the COVID-19 rapidly spreading in his prison doesn't clip his wings.

P.S. Some breaking good news about Bill. He's in love! I found him a nice girlfriend, or rather my blog did, which Mary reads faithfully. They both called to thank me and said they're now a "couple," although a socially distant one, as she lives in California at least until next month, when this results in what we all long for these days—a happy ending!

ONLY DAYS LEFT, MR. PRESIDENT, SO BE BRADY! THROW CRISIS MANAGEMENT TD PASSES TO QUELL FALLOUT FROM CAPITAL CHAOS YOUR RHETORIC INCITED

January 11, 2021

After you urged that mob so forcefully to "fight" and march on the Capitol, you need emergency crisis management. What happened afterward is a despicable event that will live in infamy to the peril of your legacy if you don't do something right away to counter the strong political tide now running against you.

You should consider trying what we in PR call crisis management. So far, you and your staff haven't done too much of it.

Yes, it was nice that you asked the rioters to go home and then deplore "the heinous attack" on the United States Capitol. It was proper to express your "outrage" over the violence, lawlessness and mayhem.

It was good you deployed the National Guard and the federal law enforcement to secure the building and expel the intruders, reminding them that "America must always be a nation of law and order."

You were right to say those who infiltrated the Capitol have "defiled the seat of American democracy . . . engaged in acts of violence and destruction . . . and do not represent our country."

That speech you made was a beginning of halting the flow of infuriating, divisive, and inciteful words and actions stemming from your side of the wall.

Millions are embarrassed for you. And for our country. It's time for you to admit you made some mistakes and say you wish you hadn't roused those animals in that gigantic crowd you exhorted to march on the Capitol.

I'm sure you didn't mean it to go as far and ugly as it did. I sure hope so. Now, you need to bite the bullet and attend Biden's inauguration. And smile, which will help to bring our country back together!

An emergency crisis management program should now be put into play. The focus should be on preserving and protecting your legacy by underscoring all the positive things you did to keep America great, while it keeps you at a safe distance far from the madding crowd that wants to destroy you.

Meanwhile, you need to show more profound remorse for those hurt and killed in that melee at the Capitol and condemn it even more forcefully than you did, not with just words, but deeds. You need to lay a wreath at the grave of that slain Capitol Police officer. And do more as part of a crisis management program.

And you need to persuade Twitter to give back your account by promising you will never incite violence. You without Twitter is like a Joe DiMaggio without a baseball bat.

But next time, not too many tweets, and no foul balls inspiring lawlessness. You need to be more careful with what you whip up.

Do this, Mr. President, and you might have a chance to Make Trump Great Again! Or at least not seen as hateful by those who seek once again to impeach you. Crisis management must highlight the best of you in a way that dilutes the media's and Nancy Pelosi's concentration on the worst.

I voted for you, Mr. President, and wrote a book about you right after your triumph in the 2016 election: *Is There Enough Brady in Trump to Win the inSUPERable Bowl?*

So I know you have it in you to veer more toward leadership, and even occasionally diplomacy when you want to. So show you are more caring about those who were hurt and killed in that melee your strong words incited, whether you meant to or not!

Now, Mr. President, before it's too late!

This one?

(Holds up Headline: "Kane Elected")

"No, I'm afraid we've got no choice."

(Holds up Headline: "Fraud at Polls")

CHANGE "ELECTED" TO "REELECTED" AND SCENE FROM *CITIZEN KANE* EQUATES TO CURRENT EVENTS

January 13, 2021

Watching the classic film *Citizen Kane* on TCM last night, I could just imagine Orson Welles licking his chops wanting so much to play a remake called "Citizen Trump."

I couldn't help thinking how much *Citizen Kane* was similar to current events or maybe it was just mimicking what's going on today in Washington.

I can see the late great actor, director, screenwriter, and producer Welles wanting to play President Trump in the worst way in a remake of *Citizen Kane.*

Sorry, I don't mean to offend the President or Republicans in general. They had every right to challenge the integrity of the last election and call out "fraud" as they saw it, felt it, or suspected it.

Actually, I'm willing to help Trump with what I'm experienced at doing so successfully for major figures over the years—crisis management.

In another incredible piece of irony, Welles attained national notoriety with a program he narrated based on H. G. Wells's *The War of the Worlds.*

Using the format of a simulated news broadcast, Welles announced an attack on New Jersey by invaders from Mars. I grew up in Atlantic City, New Jersey, so it doesn't surprise me, as I remember seeing guys acting like extraterrestrial jerks chasing girls on the boardwalk.

Reports rang out that Welles's program caused a nationwide panic. They were somewhat exaggerated, but it did serve as a launchpad for Welles's spectacular film career.

The reports of panic reminded me of that brazen attack on the Capitol, where the grotesque, ugly scenes caused genuine panic. Yes, unfortunately, they were not exaggerated, but real and disgusting.

Now, I'll close this with a Welles quote, which also may be prophetic: "If you want a happy ending, that depends, of course, on where you stop your story."

IS THE COVID VACCINE COMING AT "WARP SPEED" OR MEANDERING AT A SNAIL'S PACE TOWARD OUR ARMS?

The vaccine was supposed to roll out to us citizens sixty-five and older at "warp speed." But I think it's coming to our starving arms more at "warped" speed, not "warp speed."

"Warp speed" means extremely high speed, but what we're seeing and definitely not feeling in our arms is a far cry from that.

The term *warp speed* comes from a warp drive, a theoretical superluminal spacecraft propulsion system in many science-fiction works, most notably Star Trek and much of Isaac Asimov's work. It's also mentioned a few times in Doctor Who.

On the other hand, or other arm, warped speed means a speed bent or twisted out of shape, typically as a result of the effects of heat or damp. Also, warped in the sense of a warped sense of humor, meaning abnormal, strange or distorted.

If you ask me, I think we've been warped.

This vaccine delivery is far from warp speed. If you ask me, it's just plain warped, light-years from warp speed.

Sorry, but that's how I see it. And all this while, don't feel it.

I call it the molasses vaccine delivery orchestrated by warped politicians.

The most important mission any president has to undertake while in office is successfully defeating an aggressor.

COVID-19 is an invasion, an attack on our country. We're at war. And to leave it up to our states and their erratic governors and cluttered bureaucracies to combat it is asinine to the nth degree.

Now, the dispensing of those vaccines is in chaos and going agonizingly slow when our country needs our professional military to see to it they get shot quickly into people's arms before the death toll mounts higher and higher, especially among our most vulnerable population, me included.

I'm afraid President Trump's legacy will center on how he dealt with the COVID-19 invasion where it counts—with shots in arms—and how he may have incited a mob to take shots at our democracy.

TRANSMEDIA GROUP TO CELEBRATE FORTY YEARS IN PUBLIC RELATIONS, STARTING WITH AMERICA'S LARGEST COMPANY AS ITS FIRST CLIENT

The international PR firm, TransMedia Group, that I started back in 1981 will celebrate its fortieth year in business on February 1. And like the iconic Energizer Bunny, TransMedia still keeps going.

Over the years, TransMedia has served clients worldwide with distinction, starting with AT&T as its first, which at the time was the largest company in America.

They're not our client today, but back then they sure were a handful as I helped the megaphone company, then headed by Charles L. "Charlie" Brown, through a monstrous antitrust lawsuit climaxing in a historic breakup—one of the most tumultuous restructurings in US corporate history.

I coached Charlie on national television appearances I arranged for him. Talk about working your way up the ladder—Charlie started at AT&T as a pole climber.

At the time, AT&T had a million employees and a monopoly over most phone service. Its breakup unleashed a wave of competition in markets for telephone service and telecommunications equipment.

TransMedia did publicity for the first cell phone developed by AT&T and for other divisions of the sprawling company including Picturephone Meeting Service, a predecessor to virtual meetings so common today. TransMedia arranged and publicized the first coast-to-coast video conference for the Academy of Motion Picture Arts and Sciences.

These days my once bloodied but unbowed PR firm is under the virtuoso direction of my talented and resourceful daughter Adrienne Mazzone. He is the president while I've been kicked upstairs to CEO and a new position I now hold, news release polisher.

Adrienne keeps sending me releases written by our young staff and interns, asking me to please polish them. And I've become literally the polisher in chief, the Wordshine Man.

Since Ma Bell, we've represented many of the largest organizations in America, including the City of New York, for which I conducted an advertising and PR campaign for fair housing that won a Bronze Anvil Award from the Public Relations Society of America."

I wrote speeches for then Kellogg's chairman Bill LaMothe, which were reprinted in the *New York Times*. Then it was the FTC seeking to break up the major cereal companies, charging they were an illegal oligopoly.

In one of my speeches, I appealed to the federal government to spare Tony the Tiger from such a heart-wrenching breakup.

Before launching TransMedia in New York City, I was the number-two ranked executive at NBC, reporting directly to then CEO Fred Silverman. Prior, I was director of PR and top speechwriter at American Broadcasting Companies.

Before that I was a newspaper reporter at the *Press* of Atlantic City, New Jersey, where I grew up, and at the *Philadelphia*

Inquirer, in the city where I was born and educated. I went to Temple University undergraduate, then to the Annenberg School of Journalism at Penn for my master's in (what else?) communications!

In 1986, I relocated TransMedia to Florida and bought a building in downtown Boca Raton, which became our world headquarters.

Our first Florida client was Rexall Sundown, whose sales of nutritional supplements we helped grow from $100 million to $900 million a year. When founder and CEO Carl DeSantis sold the company for $1.6 billion, he credited TransMedia for generating media exposure that made his supplements superlative.

Thank you, everybody. It's been fun! And thank God—just like the Energizer Bunny, Kellogg's Corn Flakes, and AT&T, it still just keeps going!

CHAPTER 11

NOW, HERE ARE SOME OF MY FUNNIEST, MOST POIGNANT BLOGS AND ARTFUL ARTICLES. THE FIRST IS ABOUT A NEW ART FORM I RECENTLY INVENTED—PANDEMIC ART

Welcome to art in plastics—recycling trash into art.

The Pandemic Playground is a surreal composition comprising a phantasmagoria of plastics my wife, Rita, and I collect each day off the public beach in front of our stately oceanfront condo, the Chalfonte.

Behold the plastic toys, buckets, shovels, and rakes. Plastic seahorses, smiling starfish, and pearly fish wearing underwater goggles. Then there are the plastic crabs, turtles, and rubber dinosaur striking fear into the faces of tiny creatures.

What? A plastic cone? So I plop a golf ball in, and it becomes vanilla ice cream.

See the assorted figurines and objects, all paraphernalia in plastics discarded and strewn about, desecrating our beloved beach, insulting our ecosystem, yet they're raw material for art.

Looking at it now artistically assembled, the once ugly trash turns into *The Pandemic Playground*, an imaginative work of art in plastics.

Collecting it has helped us to stay sane during this prolonged pandemic while paying our respects and artistic homage to our planet—to our besieged environment befouled and desecrated by billions of plastic bottles and caps, knives, forks, and spoons.

Why do restaurant workers continue to automatically toss those packages of plastic utensils into curbside orders? Why do kids leave so many shovels in the sullied sand? After a day's sandcastle building and hole digging, why can't parents see to it that the plastics are collected off the beach?

And now making things worse we're seeing heaps of discarded face masks washing up on shores worldwide. Oh, our poor planet!

One of the several works of art I drew from the playground, created and signed with my artist's initials, is a collection of different colored plastic shovels we collected from the beach. The work is titled unsurprisingly, *Shovels.*

If a museum would like to exhibit it, I'll gladly supply this original work of art.

ONE OF MADOFF'S VICTIMS WAS MY LATE FRIEND, THE LEGAL MASTERMIND AND PICASSO LOVER, MEL WEISS

I couldn't help writing to one of my favorite columnists, Bill Bonner, who asked in his *Diary* column last week for a moment of silence. It was for the passing of Bernie Madoff, architect of the largest Ponzi scheme in history, who died last week in prison. Here's what I wrote to Bonner to where he's perched in Youghal, Ireland, as his column rang another bell fondly in my muddy, money memory.

Bill, your Diary *column on con man Bernie was almost biblical—only Madoff was a Robin Hood who took from the rich and gave to the richer, noble like Chernobyl, but he paid his debt in spades, poor guy. One of his Ponzi victims was a pal of mine, Mel Weiss, who lost millions following, and I guess betting on, Madoff.*

Mel ran one of the largest class action litigation law firms in the United States, winning hundreds of millions in judgments for clients scammed, screwed, and robbed, until he himself got screwed and had to endure a lot of legal folderol after his law partner sold him out for breaking an oblique, esoteric law that only exists in America. But to me and the millions who benefited from his brilliance, Mel will always be a hero!

Poor Mel succumbed to ALS in 2018, leaving behind still many more millions, along with one of the largest private collections of his favorite artist, Picasso. Mel rented an office from me in a building I own in downtown Boca Raton, Florida, and one of the highlights of my day would be when he'd mosey over to my boardroom to say a few trenchant words as I was pitching a prospective client for my public relations firm, TransMedia Group.

If it's true that you're judged by the company you keep, Mel would always make me look owlishly wise when he popped in and helped me plead my case that I was the world's greatest spin man—the title of one of my books I was honored to autograph for my dear departed friend and fellow owl, Mel, who once drew a picture of me (see below).

I told Bonner I'd be coming to Ireland with my beautiful Brazilian wife Rita one of these days after she gets her second shot and would love to have drink with him, maybe a couple.

Though I'm half Irish, I've not been to Ireland and am looking forward to visiting where half of me is from—probably the better half, as one of my favorite writers is George "Bernie" Shaw. Meanwhile, I told Bill to keep up his wonderful writing!

Here's a picture Mel once drew of me.

WHY HONOR SECEDING STATES THAT FOUGHT FOR SLAVERY? LET'S RENAME DIXIE HIGHWAY AFTER A HEROINE WHO RISKED EVERYTHING FOR FREEDOM!

The long road to Harriet Tubman's name replacing Dixie Highway is now a longer, lonelier road without Coral Gables supporting it in Miami-Dade County, Florida. So how about we rename it Harriet Highway!

Why? Slaves were not legally allowed to marry in 1844, so Harriet just entered a marital union with a free Black man, John Tubman, while giving herself the name Harriet. As she bravely helped slaves escape to freedom, her husband refused to join her and remarried a free Black woman.

Known as the Moses of her people, Harriet was enslaved, escaped, and helped others gain their freedom as a "conductor" on the Underground Railroad. Harriet also served as a scout, spy, guerrilla soldier, and nurse for the Union army during the Civil War. She is also considered the first African American woman to serve in the military.

So, in the name of the equal rights and freedom for which she so devoutly fought, I vote we put Dixie Highway up on a higher road with the new, more alliterative handle, Harriet Highway.

Meanwhile, Miami-Dade County backers of renaming the state road face setbacks in Tallahassee and Coral Gables.

Coral Gables is the only local government in Miami-Dade to reject adding Harriet Tubman's name to forty-two miles of US 1, a federal and state road which has been called Dixie Highway for a century.

County commissioners endorsed the switch last year from a name often linked with the Confederacy and racism to the name of the country's most famous "conductor" on the Underground

Railroad network used to free enslaved Americans before the end of the Civil War.

Passed unanimously in February 2020, the county resolution only created Harriet Tubman Highways off a few Miami-Dade roads that run along US 1, which carried the names "West Dixie Highway" and "Old Dixie Highway."

Swapping "Harriet Tubman" for all of "Dixie" on US 1 itself requires a state process that could take years, allowing businesses along the highway time to update letterhead and promotional materials with the new address, which I'm sure many would gladly do.

But first the Florida legislature needs to approve the change. With just two weeks left to go in the 2021 session, supporters are not very optimistic.

"Right now it's stalled. Dead," said Senator Shevrin Jones, the West Park Democrat who is a sponsor of the Senate version of the legislation SB 1216.

"We'll have to do it again next year," the *Miami Herald* quoted him saying.

I can hear Harriet and all those ex-slaves she helped applauding from heaven.

ONCE AGAIN HOLLYWOOD NEEDS TO COME OUT AGAINST HESITANCY

Posted on April 22, 2021 by maddenmischief

Hey Hollywood, America needs you once again if we're ever going to reach that safe zone called herd immunity. You need to come out strong against hesitancy.

Back in the 1960s, it was Hollywood stars like Elvis Presley who flashed their iconic smiles and stuck out their arms to counter trypanophobia, an irrational fear of injections or hypodermic needles.

Today it's surging again as thousands of people are leery about joining the herd. They're afraid of getting vaccinated after an infinitesimal percentage of women developed blood clots from their Johnson & Johnson shots. It's so irrational as tens of millions of us have breezed through vaccinations without a hitch and are now protected from COVID-19.

But to stay safe, we need 80 to 90 percent of our population vaccinated.

Yet today there are vestiges of that same fear in people today who'll need to be coaxed or persuaded that vaccines available are not only effective, but astoundingly safe.

Back in the 1950s, the Salk vaccine against polio had just been produced and millions of young children were being vaccinated. Teenagers, who were also vulnerable to polio, however, were not taking up the vaccine.

So New York City Department of Health launched a massive publicity campaign to promote vaccination against polio. The following year nearly one million New Yorkers were vaccinated, and the number of new cases declined sharply.

ELVIS TO THE RESCUE

A highlight of the campaign occurred backstage at CBS Studio 50 before an airing of *The Ed Sullivan Show.*

It was there that New York City commissioner of health Leona Baumgartner held the arm of Elvis Presley as Assistant Commissioner Harold Fuerst administered the polio vaccine to the

King of Rock and Roll, Elvis Presley. And so Elvis was recruited to boost teenager take-up of the polio vaccine.

In 1963 the health commissioner at that time announced that vaccination had reduced the number of new cases in Gotham to zero.

It was one of Presley's most valiant ventures. The king of rock and roll had just been enjoying his success with singles such as Heartbreak Hotel, when he was given that unexpected medical challenge. Would he agree to be vaccinated against polio in front of the press before the show? He did.

The resulting photographs were published in newspapers across the United States. "Presley Receives a City Polio Shot," announced the *New York Times.*

The publicity worked in closing the "immunization gap" that exists between those who get vaccines for diseases and many today fearful of taking a shot that will help to protect us all in what's called "herd immunity."

So perhaps President Biden better start recruiting some rappers and other singing stars, Hollywood movie and TV stars and other celebrities to roll up their sleeves, smile at the cameras, and take one for the team.

If not, many of us might wind up checking into the Heartbreak Hotel.

CHAPTER 12

WARNING! THIS MIGHT SCARE YOU

One of the most effective attention-getters is warnings. Have you ever passed a warning sign without reading it? No, we tend to take notice of danger signs about what's ahead that might hurt us or cost us our lives. Warnings are concerning, whether it's a severe storm heading our way or potholes or worse: sinkholes dead in front of us. So this is how I got people to read about a short story published in 1948 in the *New Yorker*, which ironically has relevance to people and events associated with today's sometimes distorted concept of "normalcy."

Warning: reading this might cause nightmares! Please don't read this if you scare easily as you might not sleep tonight. It's a horror story with present-day relevance in certain parts of our polarized country and places where vestiges of racism and violent tendencies are still lurking.

WAS "THE LOTTERY" FRIENDLY OR TOO HORRIBLE TO FATHOM?

A short story called "The Lottery," written by Shirley Jackson in the *New Yorker,* unleashed a storm of protest from readers in 1948.

The uproar was in reaction to how benign and commonplace she described a friendly village where each year stoning your neighbor to death was as routine as scratching a lottery ticket in a Publix Supermarket.

Children would start gathering pebbles and rocks, making small piles of them for the upcoming festivities.

The unlucky neighbor stoned was the single loser in an otherwise convivial social event called the lottery, which was a routine, almost joyous occasion that brought all the folks together in a public square to see who would be the next stone-ee.

It was almost like today would be hanging out with a group of unvaccinated friends, embracing each one without your mask on, then going home to kiss your grandparents a loving goodbye.

It showed how depravity can seem so normal in certain societies like it must have been for children of plantation owners in the South in the early 1800s watching slaves pick cotton in the fields. Yes, it was the normal thing to do back then in the segregated south.

Or today watching a white cop kneel on a Black man's neck seems almost routine and normal, just like for poor people living on a meager dole in ghettos, where depression and violence appear just like a normal response to life's extraordinary challenges.

It's like the war on drugs declared fifty years ago by a president who soon thereafter was accused himself of crimes, forcing him to resign in disgrace and to this day leaving the United States mired in a deadly opioid epidemic that did not abate during the coronavirus pandemic's worst days. So it's highly questionable whether anyone won the war on drugs or, for that matter, wars like those in Vietnam or Afghanistan.

Yet the loser in the war on drugs is clear: millions of Black and Latino Americans, their families, and their communities, especially with the imposition of mandatory minimum prison sentences and harsh federal and state penalties that strengthened the prison industrial complex that saw millions of Americans, primarily those of color, locked up for eternities and shut out of the American dream.

No, "The Lottery" is hardly a sign of inequality, social injustice, or systemic racism. It's just the way things are, so enjoy it and be curious to see who draws the next losing ticket.

The story in the *New Yorker* provoked more letters to the editor than ever before. Many of them vehement, as shocked readers expressed outrage to bewilderment. They were perturbed or puzzled by "The Lottery!" Some said they were scratching right through their scalps trying to fathom it.

"The Lottery" presented life and death as a random drawing. What cards we're dealt can mean whether we stick around or go underground.

As if life itself is a drawing for a certain skin color or having parents with hopefully a sizable net worth. We each draw what talents we'll have to develop. How bright we'll be. And most importantly, what country will be our beloved birthplace!

The *New Yorker*'s Kip Orr, who was charged with responding to all the letters on Jackson's behalf, echoed this position in his standard formulation: "Miss Jackson's story can be interpreted in half a dozen different ways. It's just a fable . . . she has chosen a nameless little village to show, in microcosm, how the forces of belligerence, persecution, and vindictiveness are, in mankind, endless and traditional and that their targets are chosen without reason."

"The Lottery" takes the classic theme of man's inhumanity to man and gives it regrettably a not so new twist: the randomness often inherent in brutality.

"It anticipates the way we would come to understand the twentieth century's unique lessons about the capacity of ordinary citizens to do evil—from the Nazi camp bureaucracy to the Communist societies that depended on the betrayal of neighbor by neighbor to the experiments by the psychologists Stanley Milgram and Philip Zimbardo demonstrating how little is required to induce strangers to turn against each other," said book critic Ruth Franklin, who wrote so insightfully about what was behind "The Lottery."

"In 1948, with the fresh horrors of the Second World War barely receding into memory and the Red Scare just beginning, it is no wonder that the story's first readers reacted so vehemently to this ugly glimpse of their own faces in the mirror, even if they did not realize exactly what they were looking at," wrote Franklin, the author of *Shirley Jackson: A Rather Haunted Life*, for which she won the National Book Critics Circle Award for biography in 2016.

FROM DARK TO LIGHT, NOW HERE'S MY TAKE ON THE CLEVELAND INDIANS NAME CHANGE TO THE CLEVELAND GUARDIANS

After being called the Cleveland Indians for one hundred years, the team will soon remove its feathers and war paint and officially drop its controversial Indians nickname.

Was it really insensitive to call themselves Indians? Was it that hurtful to our Native Americans for a baseball team to have that moniker? I guess so. But could the hurt and insult it apparently caused have been dealt with differently?

As a crisis manager, I probably would have advised them to scrap the name if it was so offensive to many Native Americans. Yet now I'm wondering if it could have been handled differently.

What if the Cleveland Indians went out of their way to benefit Native Americans? Salute them. Cheer them. Honor them!

What if the club and their fans donated sizable amounts to improve their health, education, and living conditions?

Are not Indians noble and their tribes deserving recognition and honor? Why is the connection with sports so dishonorable? Could not their honorable chiefs have thrown out first pitches?

I would have gone to my friend, actor, writer, and performer J. Reuben Silverbird, who is of Navaho and Apache descent. I would have asked his advice on how they could have made that name palatable and a win-win for all and thereby preserve a piece of sports history.

Once I helped Silverbird name a restaurant he opened in Manhattan, one of the first to serve Native American food. I suggested he call it "Silverbird," which he did, and I remember the staff beating tom-toms at the tables and serving delicious rattlesnake.

Cleveland continues to play as the Indians this season as it worked on finding a new name for the franchise.

After months of deliberation, Cleveland's Major League Baseball team declared its new name will be the Guardians. The change will take effect after the current season.

The team decided last year that it would shift away from Indians, the name it has used since 1915, because it is considered offensive to many Native Americans and others who are opposed to the use of Native nicknames and mascots for sports teams.

Thus, they followed the Washington Football Team, which dropped the name "Redskins" last year.

The club engaged in an extensive outreach program with some forty thousand fans to find the new name and conducted interviews with community members and team staff.

The name has some resonance with Ohio residents who regularly cross the Cuyahoga River on the Hope Memorial Bridge. Two massive stone sculptures on the pan are known as the Guardians of Traffic and are said to be symbols of progress.

Well, hello, Guardians. Goodbye, Indians. Frankly, I'm sorry to see you go.

MY BRANSON MOMENT LOOKING DOWN FROM MY THEN "SPACECRAFT" AT THE EARTH'S CURVATURE FORTY-ONE YEARS AGO

Not too many of us have had their Richard Branson moments looking down at Mother Earth from near the edges of outer space.

I had mine one unforgettable day back in 1980. That's right, 1980.

I was on a supersonic Concorde flight returning from Europe. We had reached a high enough altitude one day to behold the stunning, mind-boggling view of the curvature of the Earth.

When I was blessed to have had that rare astronaut experience, it didn't cost $200,000 a ticket like it does today on Virgin Galactic.

But man did I get into a mess of trouble at NBC for what it did cost back then when I was vice president, assistant to the president. My illustrious boss, Fred Silverman, is sadly no longer with us, cranking out those winning sitcoms.

The CFO of NBC at the time called me one day on the carpet at 30 Rock.

He said how dare I spend my entire month's expense allowance to fly on the Concorde back from my assignment in Europe, where I was producing a promo reel, "The Making of *Shogun*," to promote the miniseries based on James Clavell's popular novel about Japan.

At a Friday wrap-up lunch with Clavell in London, he asked, what was my hurry to get back? He suggested I spend part of the weekend in Paris and then take the Concorde back from there on Sunday. In three hours, I'd be back in New York.

Hmm. Sounded like a plan. So on I went to one of my favorite cities.

On that auspicious return flight aboard the Concorde, I sat next to the famous writer and producer of *All in the Family*, Norman Lear. The series aired on CBS and then on ABC, where I was writing Silverman's speeches before he jumped ship to become CEO of NBC, taking me with him.

That series was the first to bring reality to prime-time TV entertainment as the lead character, Archie Bunker, played by Carroll O'Connor, was a loudmouthed, uneducated bigot who believed in every stereotype he ever heard. His wife, Edith, played by Jean Stapleton, was sweet, but not the sharpest knife in the drawer.

Lear and I were chatting about this and other TV series he created when the pilot interrupted with an announcement I'll never forget.

The Concorde had just passed the continental shelf of Europe when the captain said there would be another takeoff. What? Another takeoff? We're already in the air!

The captain then said to sit back with our seat belts on and expect to feel some centrifugal force. And man, did we ever!

It was just like the first takeoff from the runway back on earth only this time we were way up in the air. It was five times more forceful, which threw you back into your seat and kept you pinned there for several seconds. It was exhilarating.

Norman and I looked down and could see the curvature of our beautiful Mother Earth. It was breathtaking!

It was my Branson moment!

I'VACTED
A PANDEMIC PLAY BY SHAKESPEARE

To mask or not to mask: that is the question.

Whether 'tis nobler to suffer the pings and arrows of outrageous Foxers like Tucker, or take political arms against insolence of gubernatorial office holders like DeSantis, those who doth spirally spurn mask mandates.

Why Gov no vaccine orders even for workers in those undiscover'd places, from whose bourn no family member now returns: Florida's old-age homes?

Go ahead, pummel thy CDC, say its science too salty, exhort thy tribe to ignore it. Then have native hues of vaccine resolution sicklied o'er with the pale cast of hesitancy!

To mask, yes, to breathe no more free air, but by doing so help end thy pandemic now deadly sharpened with COVID variant our flesh is heir to. 'Tis this not a consummation devoutly to be wished?

No more sleep with ventilators in ICUs where what dreams may come to young, unvacted before they shuffle off their mortal coil. Must not this give us pause?

For who would face masks bear, to grunt and sweat under bleary eyes? But that the dread of death makes us rather bear those chills we have than fly to others we know not of.

Thus COVID doth make cowards of us all, but how much better than to die, to sleep, perchance to dream . . . why was I such a fool to not have proclaimed: *i'vacted.*

THE LAW OF PURPOSEFUL PR

To be successful in public relations, messages need to be deliciously to the point, satisfyingly substantive, and most of all, *purposeful*!

I tell this to my staff all the time at TransMedia Group on purpose!

To get the point that without proselytizing, cloaking intent, trying to razzle-dazzle, or sugarcoat, PR messages must be imbued with clear and obvious purpose. Intent!

Send opaque, poorly crafted, non-newsworthy, or self-centered messages to media, and you'll come off like a proud preacher without goals or conviction . . . a soused singer performing wearing a face mask . . . a clumsy marionettist who's all thumbs.

Motives need to be boldly transparent. Open. What do you want the recipient of your message to do? Buy something? Go somewhere? See something? Say it!

Want to make someone feel good about a happening? Tell them precisely why they should feel that way. Why they should support a candidate, approve a platform, donate to a charity, embrace an ideology?

And don't take your time. Do it right off. Don't beat around that proverbial bush. News releases, media pitches, emails, tweets, posts, and almost all forms of PR communications must be *purposeful* right out of the gate.

That purpose needs to pop and be stated clearly right off the bat. Recipients of your message should see your purpose right away.

What do you want them to do? Buy something? Invest? Know more about an event? Feel good about what's just happened?

Time is precious. Your purpose needs to leap out from the very beginning as the recipients of your message want to know what you're espousing, selling, explaining, exhorting, or clarifying. And their time and tolerance is short.

Tell them right in the headline or first couple of sentences. Who has time to figure out what you're driving at? Or wait for a trainload of words? Certainly not reporters who receive tons of messages from PR people trying to be clever, witty, or likeable.

But's where the beef? In this case, where's the meat, the substance, or the essence of your message? Or these days, where's the plant-based meat substitute?

Don't lead with a soft bun. Lead with high-protein facts.

That first bite of your message better be objectively clear. Sure, tasty helps. No one wants to dip into something when the first bite is sour, silly, or abstruse. So it better be beefily obvious. Deliciously to the point! Right from the get-go, hits a bullseye!

CUOMOPHOBIA, OR JUST CALLING IT LIKE IT IS?

In another time or place, perhaps it wouldn't be quite as bad, but not today. No sir, not now with so many women coming out with similar stories of the New York governor's alleged indiscretions.

Governor Cuomo's biggest mistake was not being a head of state during the Renaissance or perhaps in ancient Rome instead of smack in the center of today's modern Me Too Times Square.

It's hardly the moment to be a wannabe lover boy or a Don Juan-esque boss. How flagrantly unfashionable and discordant that is amid women in the workforce having had their fill of groping galoots as over-privileged bosses.

There have been many versions of the Don Juan story, but the basic outline is he was a wealthy libertine who devotes his life to seducing women.

In Governor Cuomo's case, he's alleged to take great pride in his ability to just be charming, kiss friendly and huggable, or what he might call being just a warm hearted, warm blooded Italian American.

The engaging Gov seems to enjoy playing the bon vivant, the sexually-inquisitive male role around women, but unlike Don Juan, he never disguises himself or assumes other identities to seduce them.

No, the governor likes to cite he's just Italian as if to say, you know how Italians are in Rome toward women, ever flirting, sometimes pinching them on the rear end as they walk by. (That's still a custom?) Or demonstrably admiring certain parts of their anatomy. Va-va-voom!

Actually, for men, fooling around in ancient Rome was legal, friendly, very public, and (perhaps for some today *wistfully*) widespread. Even Roman men of the highest social status were free to engage women for love without incurring moral disapproval, so long as they demonstrated self-control and moderation in the frequency and enjoyment of such acts of pleasure.

Latin literature portrays readily obliging women as plentiful in those sordid times, but today women are strikingly (better believe it, bud) different!

Most women today are straight arrows whose minds are on work, not play . . . on achieving, not serving or pleasing the CEO—that is, if they haven't deservingly risen to that rank themselves.

Modern working women today are through with being treated as just playthings in offices or managed and manipulated by older men in power in Hollywood.

So men, especially governors and presidents, particularly ex-presidents, better treat all women with utmost courtesy, respect, and appreciation.

Or governors, they will have your ass!

TIPS ON PREPARING FOR THAT ALL-IMPORTANT NEWS CONFERENCE OR MEDIA INTERVIEW

Take it from the spin man himself, Tom Madden, who has prepped America's top CEOs for the most important interviews of their careers; here's how to make your next interview a contender for a PR gold medal.

First, Fear Not!

An interviewer on a news program can spot right away if you're anxious about a topic or uncomfortable with a question, so fear not.

Be Disarming

Many executives fear being pummeled by the press, surprised by trick questions, confronted by adversarial or controversial interviewers like Chris Wallace's dad, Mike Wallace, as he used to do on *60 Minutes*.

These fears often raise the question: how can I control an interview? Answer: you can't! But no matter how rough the waves, you can always steer into calmer, more accommodating waters.

You want to disarm your sometimes marauding interrogator by flashing the surest sign of truth and confidence—your smile. Answer even the most annoying question as if your inquisitor were your lovable grandson whom you sometimes have to patiently, but ever so sweetly, correct.

Watch Out for Ambush Interviews

Often media like to ambush, catch you off guard, make sparks fly. How to control interviews are major concerns of those about to face news media, especially during crisis situations. We often picture intense questioning almost like an interrogation, but often an ambush interview can be subtle and not as easy to notice at first. You need to be able to detect the signs of an ambush interview so you can be prepared.

Venues such as trade shows, conferences, public meetings, and marketing events are all places where you may have one-on-one discussions with someone, who just might be a reporter. Also, be on your toes, because sometimes a reporter could be in a group. You may not find out until they start asking questions, yet it's never too late to temper your remarks.

Best policy is to avoid saying anything that would embarrass you or cause problems for your company if you were quoted the next day in your hometown newspaper or on local TV. The key is to limit your statements on TV or print interviews to just want you'd like to see reported. In other words, say what you would want to see on TV as a sound bite, or as a quote in newspapers or on social media.

Steer Interviews in Your Direction

Trying to control the interview is not always the best way to go about getting good press. It can even be counterproductive.

Controlling an interview can be difficult and sometimes impossible. You can't control the questions the media asks or how the reporter will write the story.

What you can control, however, are your own emotions and the words you speak and the points that you make. The best way to approach an interview is to be alert for opportunities for delivering (or slipping in) critical messages that you'd like to get out.

For TV interviews, I always tell my clients to think of three things they'd like viewers to remember from an interview. So go in with a strategy to plant those points, regardless of what questions the interviewer asks. Yes, you're obligated to answer specific questions, but then you can divert to content you wish to impart. Also, don't just say "I" or "we" without repeating your company's name a few times—for example, "We at Aqueduct Plumbing believe it's never too soon to fix a leak."

To see entire media training tips, go to the TransMedia Group website: transmediagroup.com/transmedia-group-media-training-tips.

WHO'D HIRE A CRYPTONUMBSKULL LIKE ME TO WRITE CRYPTOPICALLY?

But I am a good writer, in case you haven't noticed yet from my many articles, books, and hundreds of blogs, but there are content limits to my eclectic nature.

So when my daughter Adrienne, president of TransMedia Group emailed me that *Coin Writer* was looking for writers for cryptopubs who would pay writers for articles about crypto in crypto, I said I wasn't cryptinterested.

While I'm sort of a cryptonumbskull, Adrienne Mazzone is the flip side of the coin currency. She has successfully promoted

Timicoin in Texas, moderated many crypto webinars, and done quite a bit of coin publicity at the major crypto conferences in Las Vegas and around the crypto country.

Now it appears cryptocurrency has brought forth a new wrinkle for writers.

With its value going in full swing, it's no surprise everyone is after cryptocurrencies like Bitcoin, but I have my hands full just shepherding my few equities, mostly blue-chip financials and tech stocks.

Due to that, finding a job that pays in cryptocurrency doesn't move my needle much, but I am curious about all these cryptocurrency platforms looking for writers, including Today's Gazette, Coincentral, NXT Alpha, and Zycrypto, a top-performing news site and platform solely dedicated to cryptocurrency.

Apparently, they're ever-eager to break news, shake things up a bit-coiny by hiring the right talent and paying him or her in--what else--cryptocurrency.

Then I'm seeing crypto consumer spending ballooning. At least, one billion dollars is the low end of what they spent in just July.

That by itself is a compelling sign for crypto. Visa, one of the biggest financial services companies, not only sees the value in crypto-connected users, but it's showing major evidence consumers are latching on.

But the breaking news is the one-billion-dollar figure just counts people who use Visa products. That doesn't include the hordes who made private transactions using crypto or shopped at businesses accepting it through a different company.

Holy CryptoCow!

So if I want to apply as a writer who'll accept payment in crypto, I'd better snap to it and learn more about crypto and why it's becoming so popular throughout the ever-expanding, sometimes contracting, crypto world.

Still, I'm wondering if I could get paid as a writer at least half in cash?

WHICH IS THE BETTER PRESIDENT: A PUGNACIOUS PENGUIN OR A CUDDLY PUSSYCAT?

You must be well adapted to harsh conditions to call the southernmost continent your year-round home.

It's sort of like that in the topsy-turvy continent called the District of Columbia.

There, it seems helpful to be well-adapted to climb steep snowbanks each day, dodge ice picks hurled at you from all directions, and tolerate transitory temperatures from freezing one day to sunny the next.

In a democracy sometimes stalled and snowbound and at times overheated and perspiring, the question is whether it's better to have a strong or weak leader.

While there are good reasons to want strong, decisive leaders, there are also intermittent dangers.

Strong leaders whom many of us admire sometimes can be emboldened to overstep what is our underlying supreme game plan for running our unique and beloved enterprise, the United States of America. It's called our Constitution.

Also, mixing strong and wrong is a deadly cocktail like tough-talking Florida Governor DeSantis opposing face mask mandates in public schools, while his state has become the country's COVID-19 epicenter.

On the flip side, a vacillating, docile, squeamish leader is a prescription for disaster and despair. Weak leaders risk losing our position as the world's leading nation: a living, thriving example of why liberty and justice for all is the right and true roadmap and the best prescription for governing and enduring whatever we face.

So which is best: a strong or weak leader? A pugnacious penguin or pussycat? An irascible conservative or obsequious liberal? Let's say what's best is a S T R E A K leader who combines the best of strong with a tweak of weak.

Strong enough to stay on a tough, now once again deadly course as long as it's working, but weak enough to see it's better to change course when it's not. Thankfully, the United States has awakened from that twenty-year nightmare in that quagmire Afghanistan. To the last minute, it's still costing the lives of our brave troops, God bless them, during an astonishingly swift and massive rescue of over one hundred thousand of our loyal friends and fellow countrymen from that Islamic maelstrom.

Overly strong leaders have difficulty first seeing, then admitting mistakes.

Weak ones are always afraid of making blunders in the first place so maybe in this volatile and precarious nuclear age, a little fear might be in order.

Once we find the right balance in our leaders between strong and weak, let's not forget about something else called term limits

They would cure what President Truman said were the two worst legislative diseases, senility and seniority. Or as Mark Twain once said, politicians are like diapers that need to be changed often.

I thank certified financial planner and Fiduciary Nancy Hite for reminding me of these latter two memorable quotes and my brilliant wife Rita for encouraging me to always balance strength with kindness and a bit of wisdom wouldn't hurt.

DON'T MESS WITH MY MASKED MAYAN

Sorry, Governor DeSantis, but I have to mandate that my precious Mayan sculptures wear masks while in Florida.

Let's put it this way, these valuable pieces have survived already thousands of years, so I can't risk them contracting COVID-19, not after all they've been through.

I've had this marvelous piece for many years and with COVID-19 surging again in my home state, Florida, compounded by your resistance to mandates, I've had to resort to my own mandates to protect these precious relics.

If you don't know much about Mayans, here's a little history lesson about who they were and what they accomplished back in their day.

The Mayan civilization was a Mesoamerican civilization of the Mayan peoples who developed the most sophisticated and highly-developed writing system in pre-Columbian Americas. The Mayans are also noted for their art, architecture, mathematics calendar, and astronomical system.

Wikipedia says the Mayan civilization developed in the area that today comprises southeastern Mexico, all of Guatemala, and Belize.

Please, Governor, allow the sculptures to stay masked in my condo apartment in Boca Raton!

Today their descendants, known collectively as the Maya, number well over six million individuals who speak more than twenty-eight surviving Mayan languages and reside in nearly the same area as their ancestors.

The Archaic period before 2000 BC saw their first developments in agriculture and their earliest villages. The pre-classic period (circa 2000 BC to 250 AD) saw them establish the first complex societies in the Mayan region and cultivate the staple crops of the Mayan diet, including maize, beans, squash, and chili peppers.

The first Mayan cities developed around 750 BC, and by 500 BC these cities possessed monumental architecture, including large temples with elaborate façades.

Anytime you want to visit me to see these treasures, I'd be honored to have you over for some squashes and beans, and I'll spare you the chili peppers, but please come masked.

Meanwhile, please loosen up about opposing mandates for face masks, particularly for our children in schools here in Florida.

CRISIS MGT. RULE 1: NEVER TRY TO REPLACE A SAINT WITH A SINNER

While I'm not the biggest cancel culture fan, in the case of dropping the chosen replacement for legendary Alex Trebek as host of *Jeopardy!* I'd say it was the right call.

The decision by Sony to yank Mike Richards as the host stemmed from racist and sexist comments the would-be saint's successor had made years ago on a podcast.

The question now for Sony is whether to keep Trebek's erstwhile replacement as the beloved show's executive producer.

On that score I would advise that since he was not fired after those inappropriate remarks surfaced, I'd let Mike keep that job as he's undoubtedly learned a lesson and his now off-camera role is far less incendiary.

As the show's executive producer, Richards helped oversee the search for Trebek's replacement before he himself was named to the position. Reportedly, he said in a staff memo that the controversy had made "clear that moving forward as host would be too much of a distraction for our fans and not the right move for the show."

He's dead right about that!

Now comes the usual Monday morning quarterbacking.

Now we have the show's fans all upset and struggling to understand how, after thirty-seven years of stability and success, a television institution and staple of the American living room could have botched a succession plan so badly.

As a crisis manager, I'd have to agree with them as it's devilishly dangerous to attempt to replace a saint with an unrepentant sinner.

Just as President Biden perhaps should have planned more for the intricacies and hellish consequences of pulling out of Afghanistan, Sony should have probed Richards's background better instead of putting Jeopardy into such jeopardy.

IS AN UNMASKED SCHOOLCHILD CARRYING A LOADED PISTOL?

Which is better: preserving freedom in schools to spread the virus or mandating face masks to thwart it?

To a friend who believes Florida governor's saying, "Let the parents decide," is a reasonable response to the public outcry for mandating masks in schools, I say phooey.

Children going to school unmasked as COVID-19 surges throughout Florida is the same as carrying loaded pistols to classrooms.

To her worries that we're slipping into socialism, I say double phooey.

My friend worries too much about the government seeking to gain power that she equates mask mandates to the 1940s when fascists in Germany ordered Jews to wear a star. She compares it to Afghanistan forcing women to wear a burqa.

My friend, Nancy, with the no-laughing face, believes our Constitutional rights are being tossed aside by a socialist leaning government bent on mandates.

She feels strongly our democracy is based upon individual rights and freedom of speech without reprisal or ostracization.

Nancy believes with all her heart that we are trampling upon liberties our forefathers held sacred when they created this great nation.

Here's what I think.

If a kid wants to walk around a school pointing a loaded pistol at his classmates, who would say it's the parents' decision whether to disarm him? No one! Yet that's the same as going to public school unmasked.

If this virus is as potentially deadly as carrying a loaded gun, then wouldn't the sooner we start issuing sensible mandates be reasonable to prevent its spread?

Is not seeing it surging everywhere in Florida, while maintaining a laissez-faire position almost the same as condoning suicide or worse, mass murder?

There has to be sensible and practical limits to freedom to do whatever the hell you please. Why? Because it's endangering, sometimes killing the other person.

Just as roads without speed limits can be deadly dangerous, there must be laws imposed for our own good, particularly for the good of our children.

Soon as the threat is diminished and the invading virus army repelled, mandates to vaccinate and to wear face masks can be quickly rescinded and a saner normalcy restored.

IS THERE ENOUGH BRADY IN BIDEN TO WIN THE INSUPERABLE BOWL?* WILL MCCONNELL INTERCEPT THE PASS IN THE END ZONE AND SCORE A GOP TD?

A zest for drama, potboilers, and brinksmanship appear innate in politicians, something they have deep down inside them that wants to come out and play!

Our political leaders don't want to just win, they want to vanquish, score a triumph, score a knockout, and pull off a last-minute historic victory, like Tom Brady, who was behind in points and down to the wire throwing a miraculous touchdown pass to win another Super Bowl.

Reaching consensus, ironing out differences with opponents, and exercising boring diplomacy. All that's academic and so undramatic. Boring!

This is the drama we're watching today in Washington as our country heads for yet another cliff, this one as steep as they get, called the debt ceiling.

Will it be lifted seconds before it's reached? Will one side bow to the other in the nick of time, sparing millions of Americans from losing the social security payments they need to stay alive?

Will they spare military veterans from losing their hard-earned benefits, millions of workers from losing their jobs while markets crash and burn, companies from being destroyed, and people's life savings from being lost?

Ah, it's a delicious drama fit for Washington.

From where does this love of and fascination for drama come?

As many of our political leaders, from the president on down, are older folks, and many have enjoyed dramatic movies like *The Godfather, Batman Begins, Star Wars*, and *Thor*. Some even have seen King Kong beat his chest atop the Empire State Building, the Hunchback of Notre Dame clutch his beloved dangling in his arms, and the many dramatically-victorious Robin Hoods, Knights of the Round Table, and the brave, undaunted Sir Lancelots rescuing their damsels in distress with the latest damsel being Speaker Pelosi.

This is drama fit for kings and queens, like King Biden, Queen Pelosi; their adversaries, Sir McConnell and McCarthy; and their emperor, his highness himself, their majesty Trump, whose election was dramatically stolen by Bonnie & Clyde.

So let the play resume. Bring on the drama, kings and queens. The dramatic ending 'tis a consummation to be wished for in American politics. On that Washington stage, drama is everything. Without it you would have ordinary, dull, run-of-the-mill management of the country in accordance with a long, drawn-out script, the Constitution.

*From the title of one of my books: Is There Enough Brady in Trump to Win the inSUPERable Bowl?

THAT'S ALL, FOLKS

Well, that's it, folks. The Wordshine Man is closing his laptop.

Hope you liked the wordshining and that it gave you a few ideas how to spiffy up your writing.

Write well, have fun polishing what you and others write, and from now on, may all your scribblings, prose, and press releases be "afters."

For these books I write—I suppose for my amusement and a bit for my legacy perhaps—this one was definitely therapeutic, as it kept me busy during the pandemic, which former President Trump said a few hundred thousand deaths ago would "disappear," yet it's still surging.

Only it was he and Melania who would disappear from the White House, while I found the perfect close for this book. Yes, I'm always looking for ideal endings. This one just sailed into my laptop a few hours ago in an email from my daughter Angel, who said, "I ordered the Madden family headstone—should be erected in four months. Will let you know once it is done."

I still have a ways to go, as my wife, Rita, just got me an appointment to be vaccinated against the rampaging virus at our neighborhood supermarket, Publix, but when I do finally fold my cards, on my headstone, the Wordshine Man's epitaph will say: "There's no way I can spin this!"

Keep these final words in mind: God gives us each gifts, but they come wrapped, and we have to open them. If only we can reject our presumed limitations and see only an endless open road with multiple lanes in front of us, we'll achieve well beyond what we think is drivable and for what we're capable as writers who wordshine.

A tribute to the power of wordshine. My article might have helped to right a wrong and make freedom of speech prevail.

HEY, DON'T BELITTLE B

Talk about being "subtle," how'd you like to be that sissy letter "b" in belittling words like "subtle?"

Can you imagine what it's like being the lonely, silent "b" in "be quiet," as well as words like "doubt," "debt," or "debtor?"

It's about as sissy subtle as a letter can get.

No, I'd want to be a bold "b" in masculine words like blast, bombshell, and belligerent, if that's what it takes to stand out and be pronounced like you're someBody.

I don't want to be a fraidy cat "B" hiding behind a "T."

So beam me up, Captain Kirk. Let me Blast off with you to another Blanet ruled by B's you cannot only see, but actually hear.

And tell Jeff Bezos he's my hero, actually my Bero, with whom I'd love to have a Beer!

By the way, I just finished reading a Brilliant Book, *The Beer Diet: How to Drink Beer and Not Gian Weight*, by Gary GreenBerg!

What a Blockbuster it's going to Be!

Bravo!

I suppose one could say I have a sort of bee in my bonnet about the letter B.

FROM MADDEN MISCHIEF TO MADDEN MUSINGS

Often when I meet people, I'm asked if I'm related to Steve Madden, the shoe guy, or the football guru and game creator John Madden.

No, but I did meet big John once at the then Bing Crosby Golf Tournament in Pebble Beach, California. At the time, I was representing Bing's wife, Kathryn Crosby, who wrote a book,

My Life With Bing, that I was promoting. When big John and I shook hands, his were so large he made me feel like a Lilliputian.

So why don't people ever ask me if I'm related to Don Madden, the cartoonist, or Bill Madden, the magician and concert violinist who started out in the violin section of the Cleveland Symphony Orchestra and wound up at Carnegie Hall?

Our dad was once called the world's greatest gypsy violinist by none other than the King of Romania one night in Sam Maceo's nightclub in Galveston, Texas. I was way below the drinking age back then living on the gulf coast with my mom and dad at the swanky Buccaneer Hotel.

Way back in post-World War II Texas, Maceo's was the one nightclub that stood above the rest offering the finest musicians like my dad, the hottest entertainers, and the chicest crowds enjoying the state's ultimate illegal gambling. The Balinese Room on Galveston Island, where my dad played, was the swankiest spot on the Gulf Coast, the jewel in the crown of Sam and Rosario Maceo's Galveston-based empire.

The Maceo brothers were Italian-immigrant barbers turned bootleggers, who ended up as gambling club owners. Their immense holdings on Galveston Island and their influence helped Galveston weather the depression far better than most cities across America.

If my dad isn't impressive enough, how about another Madden, my brother Don, who is probably the greatest living cartoonist. His full-page cartoons graced every issue of *Playboy* magazine for fifty straight years. Don is a master at drawing the most colorful and the funniest cartoons you ever saw.

And me?

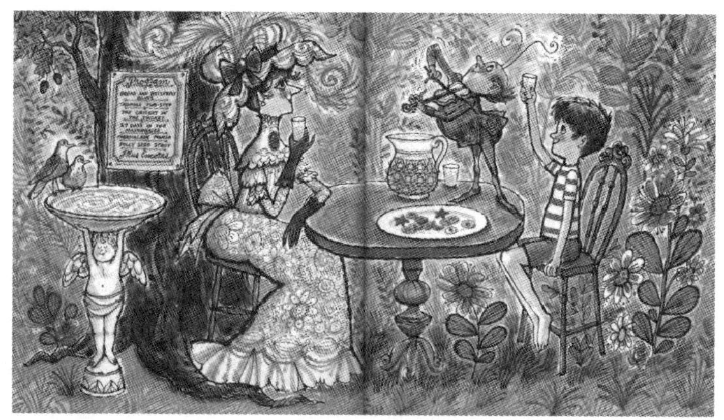

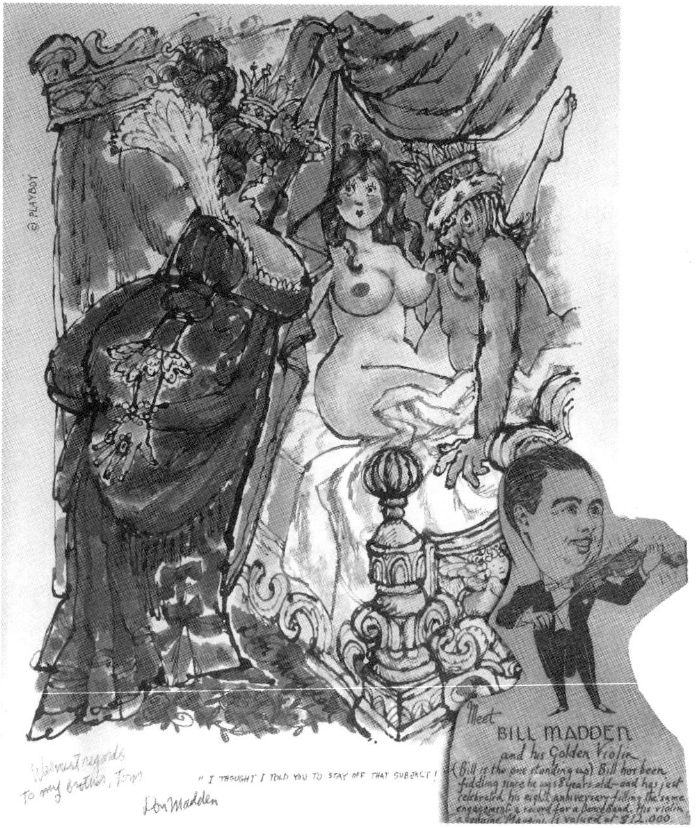
© PLAYBOY
"I THOUGHT I TOLD YOU TO STAY OFF THAT SUBJECT!"
Warmest regards
To my brother, Tom
Tom Madden
Meet
BILL MADDEN
and his Golden Violin
(Bill is the one standing up) Bill has been fiddling since he was 8 years old—and has just celebrated his eight anniversary filling the same engagement a record for a Band Band. His violin

I'm a public relations guy—a promoter—and right now I'm promoting a crop of Maddens whose talent deserves wider attention, more recognition, and greater acclaim.

So next time someone meets me, hopefully they'll ask, "Are you by any chance related to Bill and Don Madden?" And I'll proudly say, "YES! You bet I am!"

After a week of controversy, I'm happy to report that the University of Florida has decided to reverse course on a decision that had barred three professors from serving as paid expert witnesses in litigation against the state's new voting law. Perhaps this and other articles published helped to right the wrong and make freedom of speech prevail! I'm honored to be on the side of freedom.[1]

HAS FREEDOM OF SPEECH BECOME PASSE AT A STATE UNIVERSITY IN FLORIDA? IS FLORIDA PERHAPS NOW BOWING TO AN EMPEROR CALLED GOVERNOR?

If not, then why were three University of Florida professors swiftly silenced after daring to offer to assist plaintiffs in a lawsuit to overturn a law restricting voting rights?

Is criticizing your state now in the same bracket as "don't bite the monarch's hand that feeds you" and "don't shout fire on a crowded campus"? Yes, political pressure forced freedom of speech to take a back seat, at a university of all places!

The professors, all political scientists, were barred from assisting plaintiffs in a lawsuit to overturn the state's new law restricting voting rights. It raises questions of academic freedom and First

1 Michael Wines, "Florida Bars State Professors From Testifying in Voting Rights Case," *New York Times*, October 29, 2021, https://www.nytimes.com/2021/10/29/us/florida-professors-voting-rights-lawsuit.html.

Amendment rights and is maybe evidence of some states skidding to new constitutional lows.

Or bowing too quickly to a modern magisterial set called governors!

According to reports, university officials told the three that because the school was a state institution, participating in a lawsuit against the state "is averse to the University of Florida's interests" and could not be permitted.[2]

It's unclear whether Gov. Ron DeSantis, a Republican, was involved in the decision, but judging from his past actions on various other fronts, it seems likely he might have played a regal role in squashing their rights to free speech.

DeSantis prefers institutions marching to his drumbeat, like his ordering local school boards to cease requiring schoolchildren to wear face masks or lose state funding. Gov. DeSantis, and others who share his views, equates vaccination passports to board cruise ships and vaccine mandates in general to the vile, despicable orders issued during the heinous reign of Nazi Germany.

Funny, the other day I suggested to my condo manager that now since those residents fully vaccinated will no longer have to wear face masks in our building, it would be nice if they could voluntarily show they were vaccinated. Someone who overheard me shouted, "Nazi Germany!"

The university's refusal to allow the professors to testify was a marked turnabout for the University of Florida.

Like schools nationwide, the university has routinely allowed academic experts to offer testimony in lawsuits, even when they oppose the interests of the political party in power. Leading experts on academic freedom said they knew of no similar

2 Wines, "Florida Bars State Professors."

restrictions on professors' speech and testimony and called the action probably unconstitutional.[3]

One of the professors in the latest filing testified with the University of Florida's permission in two voting rights lawsuits against Florida's Republican-led government in 2018. One suit forced the state to provide ballots written in Spanish for Hispanic voters. The other overturned a state-imposed ban on early voting polling places on Florida university campuses.

But university officials reversed course after a coalition of advocacy and voting rights groups sued in May to block restrictions on voting enacted this year by the Republican-controlled state legislature.

Among other provisions, the new law sharply limits the use of ballot drop boxes, making it harder to obtain absentee ballots, and places new requirements on voter registration drives. Plaintiffs argue that the law disproportionately limits the ability of Black and Hispanic voters to cast ballots.[4]

In a letter to university officials, the legal director of the American Civil Liberties Union for Florida's branch noted DeSantis had signed legislation this year requiring universities to annually assess the state of academic freedom and ensure that students hear a variety of viewpoints, including those with which they disagree.

Barring the professors' testimony would seem to go against the grain of those very tenets, the ACLU noted. The university "simply should not be looking to Governor DeSantis to decide which speech activities it will engage in," the letter added. "That

3 Wines, "Florida Bars State Professors."

4 Wines, "Florida Bars State Professors."

is precisely the opposite of the values that universities are thought to stand for."[5]

While I agree with Gov. DeSantis on many other issues and feel terrible about what his brave wife, Casey, is having to contend with and pray that she'll beat her breast cancer, I still say this involving free speech: three cheers for the ACLU!

And now, to finally put this book to bed, here's my final piece about Governor Huckabee and Relaxium® SLEEP.

HUGGERS ARE AN ENDANGERED SPECIES THANKS TO COVID

First, let's review what that foregone, antiquated greeting was like back in the late twenty-first century, as by now many have forgotten what a hug is, thank goodness.

In olden times back on a place called Earth, a hug was a term that described a practice when two earthlings would meet and greet one another expressing fondness, or what was once quaintly called "love."

These earthly inhabitants would express this by putting their arms around each other above their waists in what is now an immoral and illegal position once known as a hug or embrace.

Often the word "warm" was used to describe these acts, yet the context, origin, and meaning of "warm" is unknown, though modern vocabularians believe it was related to having a fever from one of the ancient virus variants that once plagued the now empty planet called Earth.

Today, such behavior is virtually unknown and frowned upon by the WCDC, WNBC, WCBS, and other health misinformation

5 Wines, "Florida Bars State Professors."

organizations and is considered antiquated, outdated, and even dangerous to the indifferent.

Hugging has been replaced by simply touching what were once called elbows, considered much safer and more in keeping with modern pandemic times once confined to Earth, but now spreading throughout the universe thanks to space ships made popular by one of the early outer space settlers like Jeff Bezos from planet Amazon.

Now there were once basically three types of people on Earth in the late twenty-first century.

There were the huggers, people who liked to hug other people, and the huggees, people who liked to be hugged. And there were the bi-huggers, who went both ways as they liked to give and receive "warm embraces" or hugs. Some called them "hugsters" as they were always trying to sell their hugs in crowded places.

The latter were considered the most wild and crazy people and back in the day, they would be arrested, tried and convicted, then transported to Hugless Island. There they would remain until their brains were hug-washed, and they were rehugbilitated to stop their lurid and depraved behavior of hugging, especially in public.

If two people had to hug, they would have to do it privately late at night in the dark undercovers or face hug arrest, criminal charges, and public condemnation.

MEIR MEDICAL CENTER EVENT SPEAKERS GOVERNOR MIKE HUCKABEE AND JUDGE JEANINE PIRRO; GREET AUTHOR AND ATTORNEY PETER TICKTIN AND HIS WIFE DEBRA.

It's always refreshing to hear Gov. Mike Huckabee speak. The last time I heard him give a speech was at a benefit Rita and I attended in Aventura, Florida, for Meir Medical Center in Israel. As usual, his energy filled the room. This was early in the pandemic before face masks became so startlingly fashionable.

Huckabee credits Relaxium® sleeping pills for his fantastic night's sleep from which he awakens full of vigor to start each new day.

The geniuses who developed and brought Relaxium® to the market are a rare couple who could pass as Hollywood movie stars. Dr. Eric Ciliberti is a handsome MD, clinical neurologist, and sleep expert who developed Relaxium®. His wife, Timea, the company's CEO, is an immigrant from Hungary who wasted no time launching and managing a hugely successful enterprise with her husband. Besides successful entrepreneurs, they're an attractive couple who could be walking (never sleepwalking) on Hollywood red carpets.

Since meeting them, I've started to take Relaxium® and felt noticeably more alert during the day. Yes, there's nothing more satisfying, refreshing, and invigorating than a good night's sleep.

Actually, many people today are experiencing symptoms of a new malady Dr. Ciliberti calls "COVID-Somnia." That's right, it's a new form of insomnia, another irritant this prolonged pandemic has created. Behind our face masks, many of us are still droopy-eyed and sleepy from not having what's so essential to maintaining our health, alertness, and probably our immune system too: a sound, uninterrupted night's sleep.

By the way, if you would like to contribute to a marvelous, wide-awake hospital in Israel that treats all nationalities, Arabs, Christians, and Jewish people alike, I highly recommend you contact American Friends of Meir Medical Center. Bruria Angel will tell you all the wondrous things this marvelous hospital does.

Among them is helping premature babies survive outside the mother's womb, as it provides newborns with the right environmental conditions to develop. But their neonatal intensive care units need more of these life-saving incubators.

Now back to sleep and to Governor Huckabee, whose energy and enthusiasm almost made him president of the United States.

The Blues

Dr. Ciliberti, known as the "The Sleep Warrior," sheds some light on light itself. Although electronics give off many different colors, blue seems to be the culprit when it comes to sleep. Dr. Ciliberti says that blue lights send signals to the brain making us think the sun is up, which in turn disrupts nature's way of helping our body prepare for sleep, preventing us from releasing a sleep hormone called melatonin.

Dr. Ciliberti says that excessive exposure to blue light at night contributes to mood disorders and depression by disrupting hormone secretion, neuroplasticity, and by sending aberrant signals from the retina to brain regions that regulate emotions.

Although many people feel that watching TV helps them drift off to sleep, Dr. Ciliberti recommends to his patients that they turn off the TV and all electronics at least thirty minutes before going to bed.

Now a final word about Huckabee. He's an inspiring leader who feels deeply for our country. He maintains that what's so lacking today in political discourse is treating each other with a sense of decency. Because we have all grown so polarized, he likes to mix in his special brand of humor with his disarming smile.

If he were to ever run again, he'd have my vote as I believe he could wake America up, so that we could accomplish much more if we truly were the *United* States of America.

That is, providing the next time we all go to the polls to vote, we get a good night's sleep!

Now, close the book, turn off the light;

I, Wordshine Man, bid you goodnight.

BIBLIOGRAPHY

Wines, Michael. "Florida Bars State Professors From Testifying in Voting Rights Case." *New York Times*, October 29, 2021. https://www.nytimes.com/2021/10/29/us/florida-professors-voting-rights-lawsuit.html.

ABOUT THE AUTHOR

The Wordshine Man, Tom Madden, started to shine early in his career as an enterprising newspaper reporter for the *Philadelphia Inquirer.* During his tenure, he broke major stories until he was punched into his next career as a prominent speechwriter for major corporations and a high-ranking television network executive at NBC and ABC.

Today he is a published author, blogger (MaddenMischief.com), and public relations executive. He is the founder of the award-winning PR firm, TransMedia Group, which has been serving clients worldwide since 1981. Telling Tom to stop spinning stories and creating media exposure for clients is like telling governments to stop spending. He is the ultimate *Spin Man*—the title of the first of his five books.

TransMedia's first client was AT&T, which played a big part in the PR firm's colorful history. As a professional PR counselor and crisis manager, Tom coached the CEOs of some of America's largest organizations for media interviews, such as the chairman of Kellogg's, for whom he wrote speeches reprinted in the *New York Times.* He also prepped the CEOs and presidents of NBC and ABC for TV appearances that moved needles in the right direction. He also helped New York City promote fair housing, for which he won a Bronze Anvil Award from the Public Relations Society of America.

Along the way, Madden helped many of his clients grow their businesses spectacularly and become billionaires, like Carl DeSantis, who credited Madden for making him "Vitamin EnRICHed" when he sold Rexall Sundown, Inc. for $1.6 billion.